Artists' Journals and Sketchbooks

QUARRY

rainbows, miracul[...]
arc.

Something compels a fourth,
widening the circle. Five,
six
float in the charged

steer of his mind;
soon
others whirl his wrist.
Seven, eight - now he's on

his toes, up, up,

rising
with the music of the
spheres.

Still unsatisfied,

risks the lot, down on his
knees. He dare not drop one
Our lives depend on it.

Lucien Stryk

GLOUCESTER MASSACHUSETTS

ARTIST **ANNE BAGBY**

QUARRY
BOOKS

*Exploring and
creating
personal
pages*

Artists' Journals
and Sketchbooks

LYNNE PERRELLA

First published in the United States of America by
Quarry Books, an imprint of
Rockport Publishers, Inc.
33 Commercial Street
Gloucester, MA 01930-5089
Telephone: (978) 282-9590
Fax: (978) 283-2742
www.rockpub.com

Library of Congress Cataloging-in-Publication Data
Perrella, Lynne.
    Artists' journals and sketchbooks : exploring and creating personal pages / Lynne
Perrella.
        p.   cm.
    ISBN 1-59253-019-2 (pbk.)
    1. Art—Technique. 2. Notebooks. I. Title.
N7430.5.P485 2004
702'.8'1   dc22   2003020419
                                                        CIP

ISBN 1-59253-019-2

10 9

Design: Wilson Harvey: London [020 7420 7700]
Jacket Design: Rockport Publishers
Photography: Bobbie Bush Photography, bobbie@bobbiebush.com
Cover Art: Lynne Perrella
Copyeditor: Pamela Elizian
Proofreader: Stacey Ann Follin

Printed in Singapore

ARTIST TEESHA MOORE

Contents

WELCOME

}Introduction

Several years ago, I picked up a blank, bound sketchbook in my studio. I had purchased the book years before, without having any specific ideas of how I planned to use it. The first couple of hours I spent with the book were aimless and random. Nothing especially important or significant resulted from that experimentation, but I noticed how much I enjoyed working in book form and decided to continue.

I sensed the possibilities of a book filled with pages that described my various enthusiasms. I was reading the diaries of Anaïs Nin at the time and suddenly made the connection between her written chronicles and the visual entries in my book.

My pages were mostly collaged, scribbled, or painted in an urgent manner. Sometimes I added words, but frequently I sensed that words were unnecessary. Each page seemed to describe a unique, singular moment in time. My thoughts poured out onto the

pages, and the little book was filled up with page after page of revelations. Although I was eager to mention my latest art mania to other artists, frankly, I did not know how to begin to describe and define this intensely personal activity. I knew that the time I spent creating the pages was rewarding and seemed to enrich me in a way that a written diary did not. The flow of images and ideas seemed to come from a different source than my usual artwork did.

My first visual diary sat on the shelf in my studio, filled with pages that contained wide-ranging subjects, from the paintings of Gustav Klimt to the lyrics of Elvis Aron Presley—in short,

anything that was on my mind. I eventually read that Teesha Moore was creating her own brand of personal pages, and she called her books "art journals." Hearing that description and knowing that other kindred artists were also exploring this intense and magical process was all I needed. I threw myself into art journaling, full tilt.

Years later, I have filled innumerable books and have made countless friends who also enjoy creating artful journals and sketchbooks. You will meet them here and get a rare look inside their personal books. Fortunately, we have all discovered an art form completely devoid of rules and absolutely brimming with possibilities. Join us!

Getting Started

*Creating
personal pages*

Where to begin? Art journals are
something that we create for
ourselves alone—not merely a self-
indulgent activity, but something
worthwhile, important, and vastly
creative and self revelatory. There
is no pressure to make them "come
out right," and the time we give to
creating our personal pages, finding
our authentic voice, and letting it
sing is time well spent. Silence your
inner critic, and begin to think of
your art journal as a companion,
a muse, a soul mate.

Start today. Pick up a blank sketchbook, gather art supplies that are familiar and available, and look inward. Express. Expound. Start with the present moment. The past and future will inevitably end up on your pages, but we all need a place to begin, and the present will serve you well. What has the day been like? Do you want to embrace it or release it? Put that on your page. Is there a lyric or a line of poetry that keeps cycling through your mind? Record it on your page. Trust that anything that is threading through your mind and heart is fair game for your art journal pages. A memory. A color. An aroma. Add color to a white page. There is no need to think of your pages as finished, resolved works of art. You are capturing a moment, a passing whim, an impulse worth saving. Best of all, you are spending time with yourself, turning your attention toward your own needs and desires. You are putting your ideas and questions into visual form and exploring and debating them.

As you look through the unique and varied pages in this chapter, think of the possibilities for creating your own one-of-a-kind visual journal. The process of keeping an art journal can be a rich and revealing creative experience as well as a remarkable and revelatory exercise in self-expression, moment by moment and page by page.

Childhood

ARTIST LYNNE PERRELLA

Collaging on mailing envelopes

Sturdy mailing envelopes provide a perfect surface for doing mixed-media artwork of all kinds. A business-sized envelope was used to create this collage, which was then glued as completed artwork into the journal. The genesis for this collage was a rubber stamp designed by Claudine Hellmuth, and the image is featured in several ways—as a large toner transfer on both the envelope and the affixed shipping tag and as a series of stamped imprints at the bottom of the page. The soft rainbow of colors was added with pastel chalks and acrylic paints, and pieces of paper lace and marbleized paper were added along with rubber-stamped imprints of a favorite quotation and numerals.

Artist's insights

1 Let splashes of color define and depict your mood. Words may seem unnecessary; if so, create symbols or icons. Doodles, scribbles, and large, expressive writing or drawing all work to create an energetic and personal page.

2 Conduct a self-interview, and record your answers on a page.

3 Build a collage file of images that you find fascinating or provocative to use on your pages, or discover the enjoyment of recycling the everyday flow of receipts, coupons, and junk mail into your artwork.

4 Collect small leaves from your morning walk, and include them on your page along with your thoughts that occurred along the path.

Shining through Infinity,
Little Star Little Star,
Growing brighter like the Christ.

Dark Planet

}

Using the natural world as inspiration

The artist lifts herself up among the planets with this strong journal spread, featuring a self-portrait, planetary icons of phases of the moon, and icy crystals of queenly snowflakes. Working on strong, sturdy canvaslike surfaces, she is able to bring painterly detail, as well as collage elements and written diary entries, to her pages. These journal pages allow her to express a creative visualization of herself as a searcher—perhaps looking into a mirror or taking a celestial path, bound for answers.

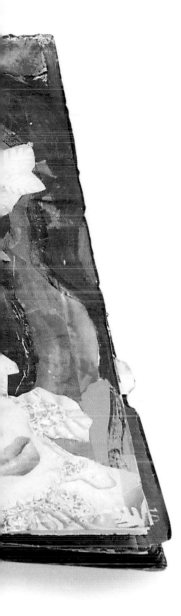

Exploring childhood as a theme

} ARTIST JULIANA COLES

} Creation Myth

Within a workshop environment, the artist leads kindred journaling souls into exercises in which the subject of childhood is explored and the visual possibilities are endless. Explore your own memories of being a child. In this colorful, textured page, the artist has used images of herself as a child to reinvent the story of her childhood, including a present-day image of herself watching "Baby Jule" in action. The lush, decorative gold-and-orange fringe, collected on a defining trip to India, brings textural interest to a page full of optimism and radiant possibilities.

JOURNALING QUICK TIP

Reinvent your childhood or affirm actual events; explore a mix of revisionist history and insightful documentation.

Art Journal

ARTIST KAREN MICHEL

Building up a base

Priming each of her art journal pages with gesso fulfills various missions for the artist. First, her journal pages begin with the brilliant white surface that she prefers. In addition, gesso gives each page the strength and sturdiness that is important for the multiple layers of color that she favors. Because she frequently uses altered books as her art journals, the use of gesso is an effective way to "reclaim" pages from an existing book. As an added bonus, she admits that the act of applying gesso to her pages also gives her an opportunity to switch into journaling mode, allowing her to relax and become ready for the self-revelatory act of

creating journal pages. After applying layers of color with water-soluble oil pastels or watercolor crayons, she used her own altered travel snapshots, using markers, watercolors, and a scratching implement to achieve the various effects, plus some collaged elements and black masking tape to provide contrast. The star motif was a hand-cut stencil, used to scrub away the background from a sheet of paper coated in blue watercolor ink. In a bit of serendipity, she later met an artist who had a collection of vintage railroad stamps, and the imprint of one stamp became the final touch to her journal page.

JOURNALING QUICK TIPS

1. To get started, prime the page with gesso.

2. Use water-soluble oil pastels or watercolor crayons to initiate the page with blended color.

3. Add successive coatings of gesso, and use implements to scrape down the accumulated surface.

4. Don't overlook your own stash of photographs to use in collages. See pages 38–39 for tips for altering photos.

*Mixed-media
art journal*

}Little
Clown

ARTIST LYNNE PERRELLA

The artist frequently uses an archival image of a phrenology diagram in her collages. Depending on its surroundings, the face suggests a continually changing cast of characters. Resembling a ceremonial figure in an Italian procession, the "little clown" is the result of numerous layers of stenciling and overpainting on a journal page that was prepped with random layers of newsprint scraps and gesso. The rough surface allows subsequent applications of paint to be scraped and scrubbed for a multilayered effect. Vintage newspaper was used to create the "hat" for the figure, and paper lace was applied as a collar. Numerals were added as a final layer, using opaque, metallic paints in a squeeze bottle.

JOURNALING
QUICK TIP

Use and reuse favorite stamps, images, and themes in different ways to push the bound-aries of their impact on your pages.

Create a source file of your favorite photographs, and make a trip to your local copy center. The possibilities for using photocopied prints on your journal pages are endless, and you will enjoy inventing new interpretations of longtime favorite images.

Working with Photocopies

1}
Experiment

Begin your creative process by making multiple prints, trying some copies on colored text-weight stock and others on white paper. Use some of the photocopies as masks or stencils; turn others into collage elements, creating various interpretations of favorite photographs and mining them for their visual drama.

2}
Use a photocopy as a stencil

Carefully cut out the woman's figure, using scissors or a craft blade. Keep in mind that you can use both segments of the stencil—the portion showing the body and the area around the figure—to achieve various effects, so always keep both portions. This piece of artwork began as a photocopy on light blue paper that was imprinted with a script rubber stamp. The stencil of the woman's body was placed on top of the artwork, and a makeup sponge was used to add acrylic paints. Experiment with offsetting the stencil slightly to get interesting outlining effects.

3}
Stencil onto old documents and letters

Apply the stencil from the previous project to a vintage letter. Sponge acrylic paints onto the surface in various colors. While the paint is still damp, use a scribing tool to add additional marks around the outside edge of the body. Apply small elements of Victorian scrap art to the dress portion of the artwork, and add a face from another photocopy of the picture. Use oil pastels to add additional color.

4}
Add dimensional items

Decorative additions to your journal pages add an element of tactile surface interest and enhance the narrative quality of your photocopied elements. Trim the artwork, apply it to a darker background, and hand-color with pastels. Glue small, pearlized buttons into place to cover the dress portion of the portrait.

5}
Use stencils for a positive/negative approach

The stencil of the woman's body was used to suggest the strong silhouette shape in this artwork. Use a makeup sponge to apply acrylics to the white background. Apply a narrow portion of the photograph to add further detail. Add patterns with commercial stencils and collage elements to complete the composition.

6}
Reuse stencils for collage

Apply a previously used stencil of a figure to a shipping tag with mat medium. Use acrylic paints to integrate the background and figure. Glue on pieces of dried plant material.

7}
Transform and reinvent an image

With a few simple stenciling techniques, this image of the woman is reinterpreted as an angel. Paint the dress portion of the photo (using the stencil to "mask" the background details behind the figure). Use a paper lace doily as a stencil to create the patterning on the gown. Apply dress details—a strip of paste paper plus a "hem" of paper lace—with mat medium. Use a circle template to stencil the corona around the head and imprint a rubber stamp of a sun overtop. Add a small portion of the face, collage style.

8}
Combine two images

This artwork was created by simply eliminating the dress portion of the copy print and inserting a vintage museum postcard. Train your eye to discover good pairings of images and interesting croppings of visual elements.

*Integrating
found objects*

}

Follow
Your
Passions

ARTIST JEANNE MINNIX

Humble finds take on the look of precious objects on these journal pages. Intense and brilliant acrylic colors combine with metallic colors to give a painted-canvas look to the pages, and the small wisps of feathers, pieces of dried flowers, bits of cellophane, and scraps of Joss paper adhered to the page add interest and texture. The verve and movement of the brush strokes, in addition to the unexpected collage elements, create a strong narrative feeling that describes a moment in time—without the need for a single word.

JOURNALING QUICK TIPS

1. Why limit yourself to one strong color on a journal page? Try them all.

2. When it comes to found-object add-ons, nothing is out of bounds. Dried plant material, candy wrappers, movie ticket stubs, shreds of newspaper, supermarket flyers, and rusted bottle caps are all possibilities. Any of these items will look like a jewel when surrounded by expressive brush strokes and strong color.

3. Location, location, location! Train your eye to discover artful and dramatic placements for the found objects in your compositions. Or take the opposite approach—toss the proposed items on your page, and allow the serendipitous outcome to continue the feeling of rare discovery. Either way, the use of unusual tactile elements on your pages will create fascinating and personal journal entries.

"Hold an image of the life you want,
and that image will become fact."
—Norman Vincent Peale

Celebrate

ARTIST JEANNE MINNIX

*Use a favorite quote
as a starting point*

This quotation provides an insight into the energetic and hopeful purpose of the artist's expressive pages. Using a full palette of vivid colors, she applies paint with abandon, allowing it to express her feelings as well as providing a messenger for her forward energy. Paint, color, and brush strokes are the strong features of these pages, but look closer and you will also discover small collage elements, as well as textured, glued-on bits of screen, metallic ribbon, and parking-lot finds. A parade of travel postcards have been cut out and combined to create a new and mythical landscape, over which a bird flies, announcing "the answer." The joyful experience of these pages is expressed in a subtle collage element that simply says, "Celebrate."

If you are having difficulty getting started with art journaling, use some of the following suggestions to add color to your blank pages. The act of choosing a color and experimenting with mark-making will give you a sense of direction and ownership of your book. It may just be the perfect "icebreaker" between you and your art journal.

Adding Color to Pages

1}
Use pastel chalks

Pastel chalks provide a wonderful way to begin a page. Shadings, from light to dark, can be achieved by "scrubbing" the chalks with a soft cloth. Combine several colors for a blended effect, or allow a single color to dominate. Remember that you are creating the beginning of a page, so random areas of color may end up being the perfect starting point. A light coat of spray fixative will set the page and prevent it from smearing.

2}
Begin with a coat of white gesso

Gesso dries quickly and provides a good basecoat for future layers, and it adds weight and substance to your page. Apply random strips of newspaper in an overlapping collage using mat medium, covering the entire page. This process will not only give your page an interesting texture but also provide you a visual element to play with when you return to create your final journal page. You can allow some of the newsprint to show or make it the foundation of a multilayered page in your book. Either way, newspaper is a classic example of an affordable and accessible art supply. Slip pieces of waxed paper between your pages if you decide to flatten your book with heavy weights.

3}
Try sponging

Sponging is a fun, experimental way to add color to your pages. Although you can purchase natural sea sponges for this task, don't rule out some other solutions. Wads of newspaper, plastic wrap, or brown wrapping paper can be used to create fascinating sponging effects. Use makeup sponges to apply paints or to dab onto inkpads. A light wash of acrylic paints over your existing sponging creates a more unified background.

4}
Create patterns

Use almost anything at hand in your studio to create interesting patterns. You can purchase specialty tools (such as those used for faux-finishing projects), or you can try using anything on your drawing table to add a pattern to your page. Working with still-wet paint, inscribe the surface with various tools. Consider using a brush handle to write or draw on the page. Save the net bags from produce and use them to create texture by dragging or pouncing them on the page. And a humble pocket comb can be used for expressive swirls and textures.

5}
Experiment with dry brush and monoprinting

Over a basecoat of gesso, drag, or "feather," acrylic paint using a nearly dry brush, leaving random strokes of paint over the surface. This technique can be used not only to prep a journal page but also to lay a final coat over a completed page to unify many disparate elements and bring them into harmony. To try monoprinting, apply random brush strokes to a piece of lightweight cardstock, and turn it facedown on your journal page, making a single imprint. This technique is excellent for creating pages with a posterlike or printlike quality. For bold and adventurous types, try turning your paint palette upside-down onto your journal page to create a multi-hued monoprint of all the colors in one stroke.

6}
Use stencils

Amass a collection of purchased stencils, ranging from the predictable geometric patterns of dots and squares to functional stencils of letters and numerals. You can use makeup sponges to apply paints. Consider overpainting several layers to create a more dimensional look. Technical drawing or drafting templates can also be used. Cut your own stencils from cardstock or manila folders. Remember to consider both the positive and negative areas of each stencil.

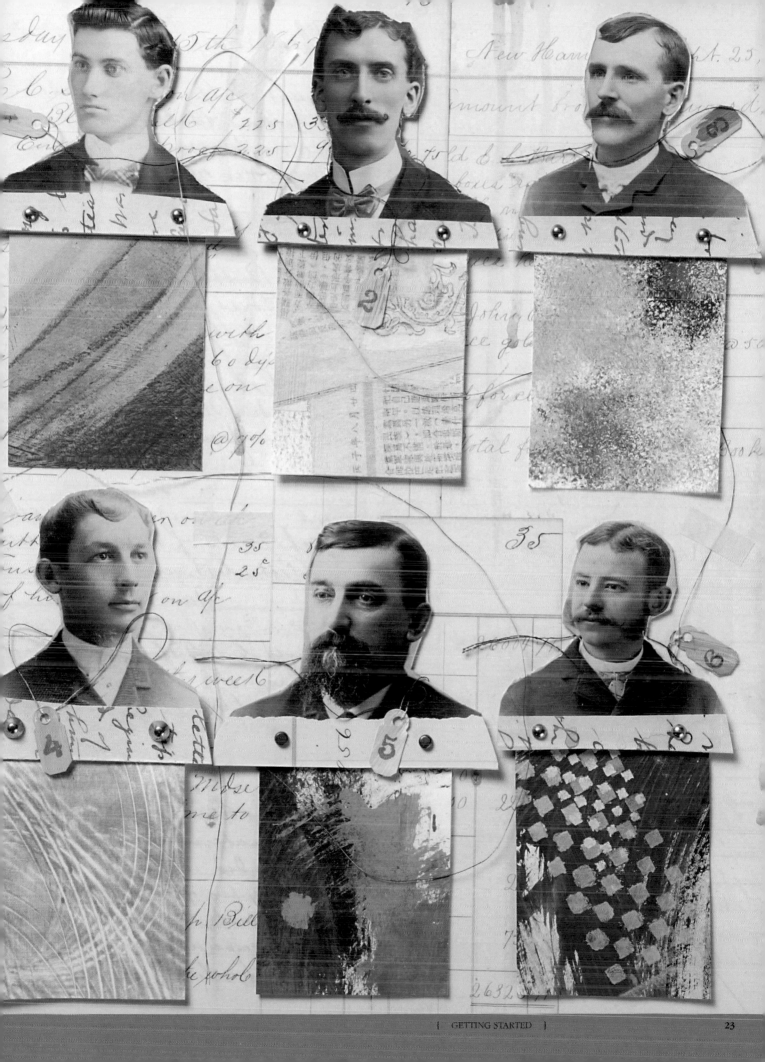

Adding Color to Pages }

{*continued*}

7}
Make rubbings and embossments

Place your journal page over a textured surface, and create a rubbing using a soft pencil or a rubbing cake. You will not only get the surface imprint but also reveal the texture of your page. Interesting subjects for rubbings are everywhere, from city sidewalks and sewer covers, to headstones in country graveyards. Try placing wedges of cardboard under a journal page and using a bone folder to burnish over the top, or use pastels or charcoal to make a rubbing of the texture.

8}
Integrate rubber stamps

You can use stamps to apply a first layer to a page or to imprint the same page, after additional elements have been added. Large-scale stamps are convenient, but you can also try using repetitions of a smaller motif, perhaps changing ink colors, and overstamping several layers. Apply acrylic paints to stamps with a makeup sponge, or use ink pads, which are available in an endless array of colors.

9}
Apply drips and splatters

These apparent mistakes provide a great way to make your pages look spontaneous and artful. If you want your journals to have the look of wild abandon, then this method is for you. If your recent journal pages appear too orderly and soulless, try spritzing them with a web of acrylic splatters. You can always mask off areas that you do not want to receive the random splatters and drips—or take a chance and let the paint fly.

10}
Use pale paint washes

Applying a watery, cloudlike wash to a page with a wide brush can be a beautiful way to begin a journal entry. You can use watercolors, acrylics, and drawing inks, all in diluted form. Also, consider wetting down a page and dropping paints or inks onto the surface. A heat gun can be helpful if you are eager to move onto the next page.

11}
Create strong, saturated color with water-soluble oil pastels

Dip crayons into a cup of water, then apply, working the color into the surface. You can also draw onto the page and then work the markings with a wet brush to distribute the color. Go back into the damp surface with the crayons and make additional marks and patterns, getting a printlike quality. This method is also a good way to add lettering to a page.

12}
Use tissue paper to create texture and layers

Begin the page with a layer of gesso, and then add random, torn pieces of tissue paper, affixing it with mat medium. Allowing the tissue paper to fall into folds and ridges adds to the surface interest of your page, and successive paint markings reveals the texture and random design of the folds and creases.

Experiment as you begin your journal pages, and remember that starting over requires only a quick coat of paint. Successful, multilayered pages are often the result of reworking a failed page until it works.

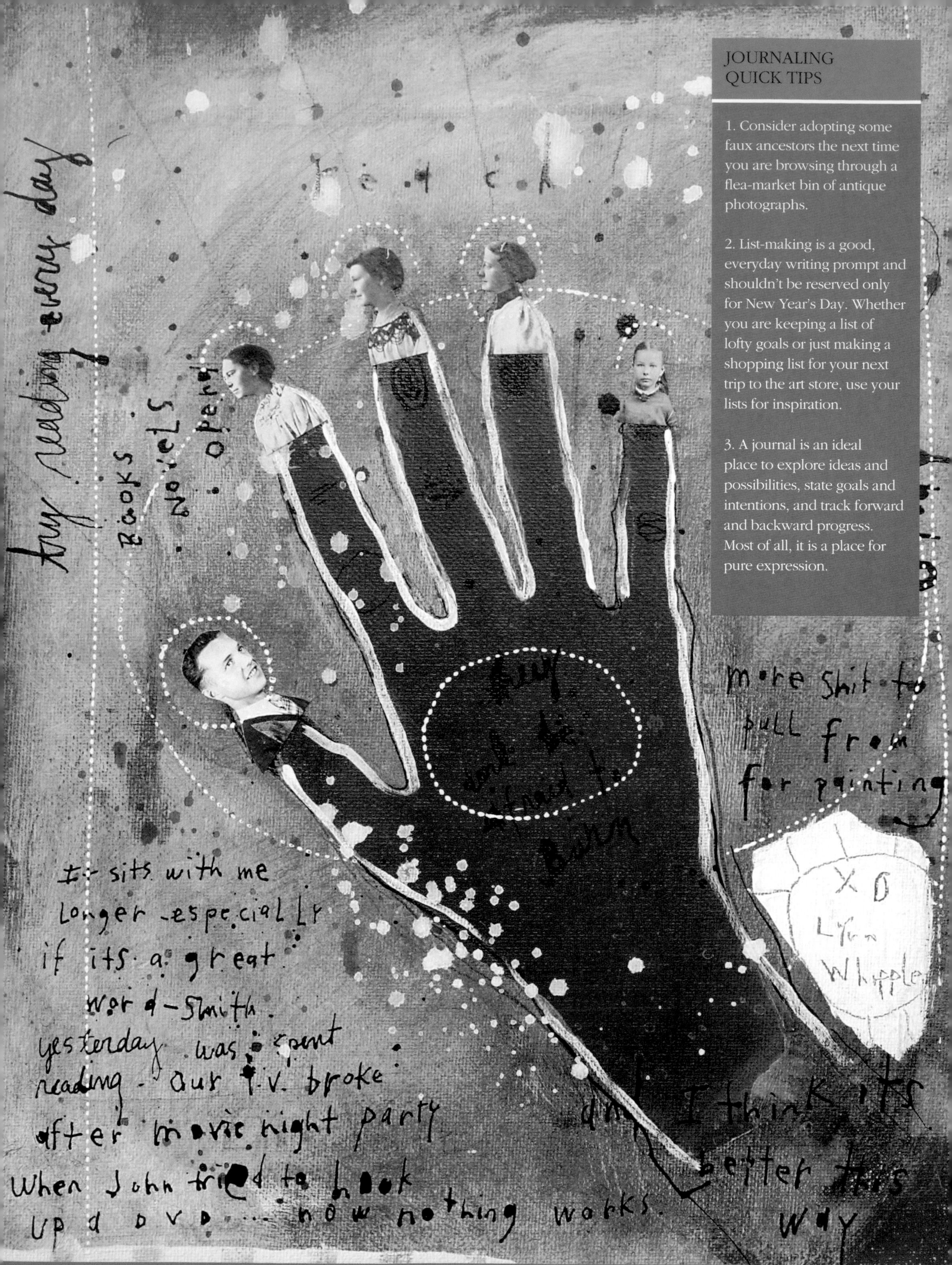

1. Consider adopting some faux ancestors the next time you are browsing through a flea-market bin of antique photographs.

2. List-making is a good, everyday writing prompt and shouldn't be reserved only for New Year's Day. Whether you are keeping a list of lofty goals or just making a shopping list for your next trip to the art store, use your lists for inspiration.

3. A journal is an ideal place to explore ideas and possibilities, state goals and intentions, and track forward and backward progress. Most of all, it is a place for pure expression.

try reading every day

Books

Novels open

more shit to pull from for painting

buy would be inclined to learn

X O
Lynn Whipple

It sits with me
longer especially
if its a great
word-smith.
yesterday was spent
reading - our t.v. broke
after movie night party
when John tried to hook
up a dvd ... now nothing works.

and I think its
better this
way

ARTIST LYNN WHIPPLE

Hand Print

Combining vintage images with contemporary flair

Count the family members—one, two, three, four, five. The definitive handprint on a canvas background gives the artist's decision to "read every day" the thumbs-up. Canvas, which provides a rugged surface for her journal pages, can hold unlimited applications of paint, ink, and mark-making; in addition, it adds a painterly quality to the collages. The contemporary nature of the strong graphic pages is enhanced with vintage photography, adding an offbeat, humane touch.

New Year's Resolutions

ARTIST LYNN WHIPPLE

The art of list-making

The year begins with a leap of faith, as well as a list of goals and visions. Because the first item on the artist's list is fearlessness, it might be a bold approach to hang her various journal pages, worked on canvas, on a clothesline in an all-white gallery. Although she works each page separately, her master plan involves creating a large volume for all her collaged pages. In the meantime, her pages provide an ongoing gallery for the beloved, old photographs from her collection, as well as a place to inscribe dreams and reminders to enjoy every minute.

Mascot

ARTIST LYNN WHIPPLE

Use your muse

Writing muse, lucky charm, and smart guy, all in one, Leonard stands at the ready with a pocketful of drawing and painting implements and all the words the artist will ever need. She used this journal page to record her strategies and dreams for future projects, including this favorite vintage spirit to serve as a witness to her plans.

All About Image Transfers

Image transfer techniques allow you to integrate vintage photographs, memorabilia, and other found imagery into your journal without parting with the precious originals. Almost any image can be transferred to various paper or fabric surfaces using a photocopy or ink-jet print of the original. (To make an ink-jet print, you'll need to scan the image or start with a digital image.) The following examples show the wide variety of results you can achieve, depending on the transfer method and the receiving surface used. Figures A through F were created by Michelle Ward on paper. Figures H and I were created by Lesley Riley onto bleached muslin. The covered buttons, Figure G, are fabric transfers by Marylinn Kelly. Each method is described below.

A} Gel medium transfer of an ink-jet print

Generously coat the receiving paper with the gel medium. Quickly place the image facedown, and burnish the image with a bone folder or wooden spoon. Peel off the paper. The ink from the printed image remains on the gel medium. Some fibers from the paper may remain and can be gently rubbed off the surface. (Modge Podge and Elmer's glue work as replacements for gel medium.)

B} Gel medium transfer of an ink-jet transparency

Follow the directions in Figure A. Transferring from a transparency results in a clearer image because the ink sits on top of the acetate and transfers easily to another surface.

C} Water transfer of an ink-jet transparency

On smooth surfaces (such as shipping tags), you can transfer the ink from a transparency with water. Dampen the surface of the receiving paper, lay the printed image facedown, and burnish well. Gently lift off the transparency.

D} Solvent transfer of color copy

Place the image facedown over the receiving paper, brush backside of the color copy with solvent, and burnish. Carefully lift the corner of the color copy to check the results, and continue burnishing, if necessary. Lift off the paper when complete. Available solvents include xylene (found in paint stripper or Goof-Off), Citra-Solv, acetone, or gin. Be sure to work with proper ventilation.

E} Solvent transfer of black-and-white (toner) copy

Follow the directions for Figure D.

F} Packing tape transfer

Apply clear packing tape over a color copy image, and burnish well. Soak the tape and color copy in warm water until the paper is saturated. Gently rub the paper until the pulp breaks up and rolls off. Keep rubbing until all of the paper is removed, and set the tape aside to dry. This process also works with permanent, clear contact paper.

H} Gel medium transfer of ink-jet print onto bleached muslin

Print the image onto printer transparency film or matte photo paper. Evenly brush some gel medium onto the receiving fabric. Lay the inked side of the transparency or photo paper onto the wet surface. Burnish the entire surface with a bone folder or the back of a spoon. Lift a corner to check the transfer. Burnish further, or lift off and let dry.

I} Matte medium transfer of ink-jet print onto bleached muslin

Follow the instructions for Figure H, but use matte medium rather than gel medium. Once the transfer is complete, apply another coat of matte medium to ensure permanency of the transfer.

G} Fabric-transfer-covered buttons

For this project, you'll need forms for covered buttons in assorted sizes. If you haven't covered buttons before, be sure to follow the instructions on the packages. You can get starter packs, which contain the pattern size and the mold into which you press the fabric and button blank. You'll need plain cotton fabric, such as muslin, and photos of faces.

1. Plan the look of your buttons by selecting images of faces and sizing them to fit. Include enough of the image to fill the entire button, plus the margin that gets turned under to construct the covered button. Make color copies of these images.

2. Cut out and paste these copies onto a master sheet of paper.

3. Copy the master sheet of paper onto iron-on fabric-transfer stock.

4. From the fabric transfer stock, cut the button cover to size using the template, centering the face in the middle. You can copy the template onto clear plastic or acetate to make placement easier.

5. To transfer, set a dry iron on the cotton setting, place the transfer stock over your fabric, and iron in a circular motion for about 20 seconds.

6. Peel the transfer stock away from the fabric to reveal your clear image.

7. Follow the directions provided in the button-covering kit.

"…[F]rom the sky, from the earth, from a scrap of paper, from a passing shape…. We must pick out what is good for us where we can find it."—Pablo Picasso

With a Little Help

ARTIST LESLEY RILEY

} *Using what is good*

The artist has reserved this apt quote in one of her art journals and has put the advice to good use. With a sure eye for knowing what is good, she has combined a handful of favorite items discovered at an estate sale, reviving the almost-forgotten faces and allowing them to speak of friendships. In pages that provide a reminder of old photo albums and fond inscriptions, the artist has demonstrated the graphic punch of a swatch of upholstery fabric underlining a quotation and a veil of discarded netting supplying a backdrop for a well-loved photo.

JOURNALING QUICK TIPS

1. If your favorite collections are languishing in drawers, try including the items on journal pages.

2. Pieces that are too dimensional for pages may work well as cover embellishments.

3. Consider taking some of your favorite collectibles to a copy center and making photocopies. "Real" and copied elements can be combined for a fascinating collaged effect, such as a photocopy of a card of vintage buttons with some actual buttons sewn on.

The artist brings her thorough knowledge of vintage textiles to her journal pages as she combines her love of fabrics and notions with page design. By keeping a collection of old volumes at hand, she is always ready to harvest selected words from these documents to enhance her collages. A swatch of fabric, imprinted with a rubber-stamped alphabet, expresses the keyword, *Know*, and a vintage portrait looks on, surrounded by antique fabric leaves and words rescued from a tattered book. A group of small, nearly forgotten items are combined with her strong eye for narrative composition, creating a dramatic and encouraging journal entry.

} Know
ARTIST LESLEY RILEY

Integrating textiles

SUGGESTED MATERIALS

Victorian scrap portraits

Vintage velvet millinery leaves

Collection of words, gathered from old books

Antique fabric swatch

Fabric ink

Rubber stamp alphabet set

These pages were created by a visual artist who constantly reinvents herself and is equally at home working in dramatic black and white or in a strong, vibrant color. She prefers handmade journals composed of her favorite Fabriano Uno hot-press paper and begins many of her pages with a wash of watercolor paints. Applying the paints directly to the page, she works the surface with a brush or tries dropping drawing ink onto a wet page. Many of her distinctive, spirited collages are a result of taking elements from foreign magazines or offbeat, used books and combining them with favorite faces from her design file. She also regenerates her pages by making color photocopies of past journals, reusing the elements in new ways. She advocates finding the visual possibilities of each scrap in your collage file—perhaps a swatch of an odd pattern, a bit of lettering from an old broadside, or an antique botanical print—always combining them for a fresh, new vision and making it uniquely yours.

Playful Experimentation

Personal pages take flight

ARTIST TEESHA MOORE

THEATRE

SOUL AT PLAY

memory of a bird

WOW-THIS PAINT RESEMBLES BLOOD. IT'S THE NICHOLSON'S PEERLESS TRANSPARENT WATER COLORS IN VERMILLION

STUFF I HAVE TO DO SOON
New rubber designs
issue number 20

cleveland show
Wholesale
journal
class
new
zines
clean
studio
finish
journals
think of
fresh new
ideas

and artfest registrations

Transformation of Gilles

ARTIST LYNNE PERRELLA

} *Sharing a work in progress*

Art journals can provide the perfect vehicle for collaboration between artists. In this case, two artists who met at an art workshop decided to continue their friendship and exchange artwork by creating a journal project based on the subject of a circus. They soon realized that the theme was all-encompassing, allowing them to branch out to include pageantry, ceremony, puppets, clowns, and politics, to name a few of the varying directions. The artists each selected a journal in which to work and exchanged the books by mail on a regular basis until both books were full. For this spread, the artist began with a favorite narrative portrait by Watteau, continuing the distinctive outline of the famous clown across the spread, using various forms of stenciling, collage, and overpainting to create the various visual transformations of the figure. Purchased stickers, rubber-stamped numerals, and colored pencils complete the mixed-media pages.

SUGGESTED MATERIALS

Color photocopy of a vintage painting

Handmade stencils

Acrylic paints

Colored pencils

Press-down stars

Rubber stamps

JOURNALING QUICK TIP

Enlist a friend to work on a joint journal project to spark creativity and play off each other's ideas.

Collaged Clown

ARTIST ANNE BAGBY

} *Telling a story*

The artist used innumerable layers of her handmade painted papers to create the rich patterning and texture of this page. Using all of the various techniques that she teaches in her mixed-media–painting workshops, she creates an endlessly colorful library of handpainted papers in every hue imaginable. Her ability to draw is evident in the minimal-but-effective details of the figure. A riot of painted paper tells the rest of the story, emphasizing the real and unreal aspects of the circus. Stitched sections of collaged papers add a fitting detail to the juggler's costume.

Angels & Harlequins

ARTIST LYNNE PERRELLA

Comparing and contrasting a repetitive image

Faces from an ancient painting by Piero della Francesca were the inspiration for this journal spread. The artist wanted to contrast two groupings of figures, depicting one as angels and the other as theatrical harlequins, to suggest the ethereal and worldly qualities of both groupings and blurring the differences. Through the use of colored tissue paper, she was able to add large washes of transparent color on top of collage elements. She also used stenciling to define the various figures as well as to establish a motif across both pages. Using many of the techniques she learned from seeing the other artist's journal pages, this artist was able to suggest the recurring figures without being literal or specific, allowing the strong use of patterning to dominate.

"He dare not drop one.
Our lives depend on it."
—Lucien Stryk

*Allowing a
journal page
to evolve*

} The Juggler

ARTIST ANNE BAGBY

Here, the juggler's story is told with a combination of drawing, collaged text, cutout lettering, rich patterning, and rubber-stamping. As these artists traded journals back and forth, both learned techniques from one another. This artist's traditional way of gradually building up a surface was in direct opposition to the other's habit of completing a page in one sitting. Both artists tried techniques from the other's bag of tricks, and this sharing of techniques was evident on the remaining pages of the two journals. Although this spread with the juggler was one of the first pages this artist worked on, the artwork went through several revisions and overpaintings until she achieved the final solution in the last month of the collaboration. The rich, layered colors are the result, and the reward, of slowly building a surface and allowing her keen eye to envision what the page needed each time the book arrived back in her studio.

JOURNALING QUICK TIP

Don't hesitate to return to a page days, or even months, later if you have new ideas to integrate.

Altering is one of the mainstays of mixed-media artwork. Although artists frequently think of ways to reinvent or change photos found in magazines or newspapers, personal photos can also be used for the same creative opportunities. Using some of these easy techniques, you can easily enhance your favorite photos, plus find ways of improving not-so-favorite photos in your collection for maximum results. Although you can digitally alter photos with various computer programs, these techniques, provided by Rhonda Roebuck, are for the mixed-media–journaling artist who wants to use hands-on ideas and work directly on the surface of photographs.

Altered States

ARTIST RHONDA ROEBUCK

Using photographs in journal entries

1}

Use a fine grade of sandpaper to gently sand around the central image, creating a vignette. Use an inkpad to add a soft halo of sepia and a metallic gold pen to create an edge for the photo. This method provides a beautiful treatment for a series of photos and is reminiscent of long-ago cabinet photos of gardens and gravestones.

2}

Use copic markers to make an ordinary, table-top still-life photo become graphic and poster-like. These markers, available in a wide range of colors, are alcohol-based and will cover almost any surface.

3}

Apply household bleach to give a contemporary color photo a historical treatment. Bleach can be applied on isolated areas, where you may want to tone down the color, or as an overall treatment, as shown here. The print was also scratched to add linear detail.

4}

Melt and blister the surface of a color photo with a blast from a heat gun. Make color photocopies of the blistered area to add an interesting texture to future collages and journal pages.

5}

Two photos are better than one—why not combine them? In this case, the building from one photograph was trimmed out, scratched and inscribed with a tool, and then added to a second print.

6}

Scratch an all-over pattern into a panoramic photo, and then use burnished-down lettering to add text.

Driving by and wanting to go in .... gate always locked .... Stay Out sign.

CHAPTER 2

The Book Itself

Examining covers and types of journal

"My home is where my books are."
—Ellen Thompson

Years ago, I visited an exhibit at the Morgan Library in New York City called "700 Years of Journals." Unlike the museum's usual exhibitions, this show in a small side gallery was not accompanied by a voluminous catalog or even a flyer listing the works of art. It was, however, an exhibit that was full of fascinating and singular journals, and I spent a great deal of time viewing them and taking detailed notes. In an enclosed, glass display case sat a stack of old notebooks with marbleized-cardboard covers. These journals were the Victorian age's equivalent of today's classroom composition books. The ordinary, unassuming notebooks were the personal diaries of Henry David Thoreau. Soon after moving to Walden Pond, Thoreau received a letter from his good friend Ralph Waldo Emerson. The note contained an innocent inquiry: "Do you plan to keep a diary?" The rest, as they say, is history.

In Thoreau's case, he did not require fine, hand-tooled, leather-bound volumes to create a lifetime of revealing and insightful diary entries. He needed merely to find the book format that felt comfortable, natural, and right. Taking a cue from Thoreau, consider the possibilities for types of artists' journal. As you review this list, allow it to provide inspiration and impulse above and beyond our suggestions. After all, the choice is up to you.

1}

Art-supply stores are full-to-brimming with blank sketchbooks and bound journals. As you make your choice, consider the size of the book, the type of paper, and the flexibility of the binding. Choices for every budget are available, ranging from sturdy, inexpensive, spiral-bound books to embossed leather portfolios with ribbon ties.

People who love books often wish to make their own. Consider taking a workshop or class in bookbinding and learn how to create your own unique volumes. In this chapter, you will see highly personal, handmade books that incorporate an artist's fascination with found objects, exquisite beadwork, and a love of sewing and quilting.

Altered books are an emerging art form and may provide the perfect option for your art journal. Paint over pages in an existing book, making it ready for new entries, while providing a unique starting point. If the idea of rescuing an old book and giving it a new life as a journal appeals to you, the choices are endless. Check library sales and used book stalls. Consider finding a used copy of a book that may have been significant to you in the past.

You may prefer to work outside of a book, on unbound pages. Virginia Woolf's diary comprised large sheets of paper, which she later had bound with covers of patterned Italian papers. Most commercial copy centers can create a spiral binding for your journal entries. What is your journal style? Do you prefer to see a neat, orderly row of your personal books on a bookshelf, each volume tied with ribbon closures? Or do you prefer your books to be wild and rangy, with collage elements and mismatched pages spilling out past the covers?

Consistency is not important. Although Thoreau never felt the need to change his custom of working in his traditional composition books, you do not have to feel limited. Many artists like to experiment with various journal types, using varying books for different moods and occasions. A small, lightweight book may be more convenient for a travel journal, whereas a large, imposing, altered antique ledger book may be preferable for your everyday, at-home journal. A loose-leaf binder (perhaps covered in a remnant of special fabric) could become a perfect gardening journal. Seed packets, magazine clippings, sketches of garden plots, and your outdoor musings can fill the pages in this easy-to-expand format. Clear plastic sheets (normally used to hold slides or baseball cards) can hold cuttings of plant material, dried flowers, and seeds.

As you look through the examples in this chapter, think of ways to include your personal preferences, interests, and visions into a unique library of one-of-a-kind books.

3}

1} ARTIST TRACY V. MOORE

2} ARTIST ROBIN ATKINS

3} ARTIST ALBIE SMITH

21

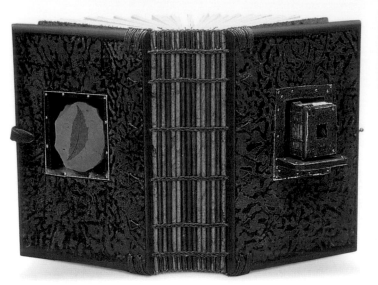

Book Shelved on Book

Book Chained to Book

Handmade Journals with Wood Covers

ARTIST DANIEL ESSIG

} "The time when books were precious objects is the place I gather much of my inspiration."

This quote from the artist illustrates and describes his passion for ancient book arts and provides further insight into this series of exquisite, hand-bound volumes. He literally makes reference to the tradition, in ancient papal libraries, of chaining fine volumes to a desk or shelf, indicating the prized status of these treasures. Although he does not keep a journal himself, the artist considers the natural objects he saves from his walks and wanderings to be a kind of ongoing, unwritten diary, and he inserts these talismans into the small openings in the covers of his books.

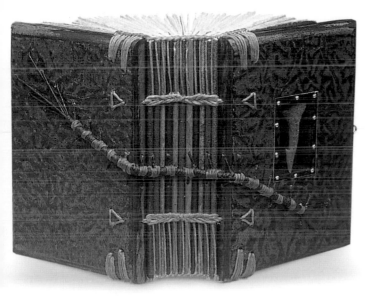

Centipede Book

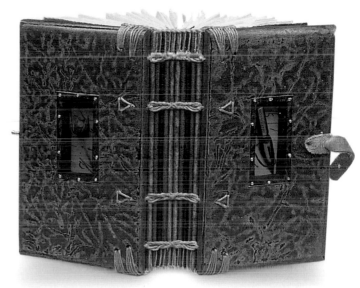

Love-Letter Book

Customize a small, purchased journal, making it the perfect book to record notes about heart and home. If you frequently look through a drawer or box of small collected whatnots and puzzle about how to use these "too good to throw out" oddities, you'll find inspiration in the journal covers on this page. These covers give an overview of ways to adhere special treasures to a cover or to create custom niches for them. The tiny key selected by the artist determined the size and placement of the opening she cut into an existing book cover. She adhered copper tape to the edges of the opening and glued a printed transparency to the cover. The house motif was made from a piece of corrugated cardboard. She also wrapped copper metallic thread around the cardboard, allowing the ridges to hold the glistening threads in place. Additional detailing in black corrugated cardboard was added with small copper brads.

ARTIST MICHELLE WARD

} Window Cover Journal

Altering a purchased journal

JOURNALING QUICK TIP

Cut out matching rectangular openings in the first few pages of the journal to accommodate a featured item, as shown here. Attach the item, in this case a small key, to an inside page using copper thread and metallic eyelets.

The humble cigar box: a fondly remembered childhood repository for cat's eye marbles and Indianhead nickels, plus a current-day possibility as a journal cover.

Making sturdy covers from beautiful castoffs

ARTISTS PAM SUSSMAN
AND GAYLE BURKINS

Cigar Box Journals

Anyone with a collector's eye for colorful vintage advertising graphics will appreciate this grouping of coptic-bound cigar box journals. The signatures of blank pages were gathered with hand-screened decorative papers. The artists used unwaxed linen to stitch through the layers and create the double-coptic spines. The cigar box covers can be collaged with other papers for a layered appearance or left gloriously unadorned, as shown. To explore some of the artists' additional ideas for offbeat book covers, check your local phone directory for a nearby metal salvage yard. Computer circuit boards, diskette holders, discarded license plates, and sheets of corrugated metal are all strong possibilities you may not have considered—until now.

Cigar Store Angel

ARTIST LYNNE PERRELLA

Mixed-media collage

Use chromolithographed and embossed cigar labels, bands, and packaging to add a sparkle to journal covers and collages, such as the one featured here. The artist has used a regal cigar band crown to top this faux ancestor, adding wisps of cigar box packaging, vintage newspaper, and bits of old correspondence to adorn the sepia portrait.

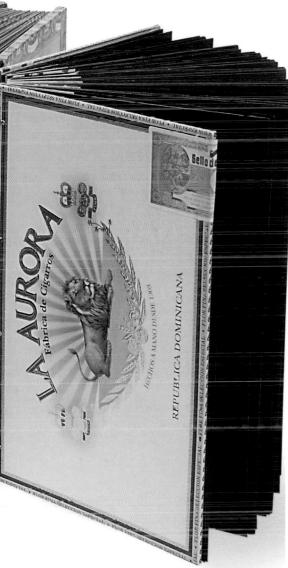

JOURNALING QUICK TIPS

1. If your bookmaking skills are limited, you can easily glue a cigar box lid to the cover of a purchased journal and add ribbon ties, scraps of leather, suede closures, or other embellishments.

2. Use cigar boxes as a readily available and affordable art supply. Some cigar stores are happy to give away their empty boxes, and others offer boxes for sale for between $1 and $5. Consider using them for assemblages, shadow boxes, and dioramas.

SUGGESTED MATERIALS

Cigar boxes	*License plates*
Circuit boards	*Scrap metal*
Diskettes	*Picture frames*
Compact disks	

The cover of a purchased hardbound journal can provide the ideal stage for the engaging finds uncovered at flea markets, estate sales, and auctions.

Achieve the look of ancient hand-tooled volumes

Elaborate Found-Object Covers

ARTIST **JUDI RIESCH**

Judi Riesch has a great eye for spotting small oddments and fragments of antique finery, and she gathers them together to create elegant embellishments for her art journals.

Her covers seem to whisper about the sepia-toned vintage ephemera she uses on her inner pages, and the volumes are decorative enough to be displayed on book easels. She takes her inspiration from museum-quality examples of ancient jewel-encrusted medieval volumes, achieving a kindred look by layering collected, distressed, and forgotten photo album covers with other collage elements. The previous closures were still intact on the antique photo album fragment. The unit was mounted onto an old embossed book cover using wire to join the two surfaces. She avoids using glue for attaching most heavy or dimensional elements, and favors the use of wire for most of these applications. A small daguerreotype frame, with part of its leather case attached, was added as a framed embellishment. Within the delicate frame, a small vignette was created consisting of an old photo, wisps of vintage endpapers, and an antique metal photo mat. Curious, small numbering brass tacks and an embossed tag were the final additions. Armed with her collector's eye, and various techniques for attaching dimensional objects to book covers, Judi has created a library of one-of-a-kind volumes, honoring the traditions of ancient archives.

Artist's insights

1 Consider old hardware items such as keyholes, hinges, letter slots, house numbers, and keys.

2 Use fragments of military medals, award ribbons, benevolent organization badges, or commemorative coins or medallions.

3 Embellish with old brooches and other dressmaker details, such as pearlized buttons or decorative braid and ribbon.

4 Incorporate antique photos, tintypes, daguerreotypes, and glass classroom slides.

5 Fill tiny glass vials (normally used to store small watch parts or jewelry findings) with objects such as seeds, pearls, beads, small wisps of paper, dictionary entries, or handwritten messages. Using wire, apply row-on-row of these tiny vials, tiling the entire front of a journal cover.

Starting with a store-bought journal with deckle-edged pages, Judi Riesch has created a journal cover completely covered in handsome brass stencils, both new and old.

Exploring the use of multiples

}

Stencil-Covered Journal

ARTIST JUDI RIESCH

Surprisingly lightweight to hold, this journal has the substantial look of ancient volumes covered in hammered metal closures and hand-tooled hinges. Use a collection of various-sized stencils (both letters and numerals) to tile the covers and spine to make a unique volume. Insert collage elements such as old documents and marbleized endpapers behind some of the stencil openings; allow the leather book cover to show through, or cover the purchased book with a distinctive fabric. Sand down sharp edges to make the stencils easier to handle, and affix the elements to the book cover using contact cement or silicone caulk adhesive.

JOURNALING QUICK TIP

If you have a group of newly purchased brass stencils, you can easily "age" them. Sand them, then paint on a coating of gel medium, and follow with washes of acrylic paints.

SUGGESTED MATERIALS

Purchased journal

Brass stencils (old or new)

Paper and fabric scraps

Ephemera: maps, marbled papers

Contact cement or silicone caulk adhesive

Once you are in the journaling habit, you may want to encourage other kindred souls to begin.

Slide-Mount Journal Cover

ARTIST MICHELLE WARD

Using simple objects for maximum visual impact

Induce them to start a visual journal by presenting them with a purchased, sturdy blank book that you have customized. This project is a quick, easy, and affordable way to turn a generic spiral-bound book into an anything-but-ordinary circus of primary colors and touchable embellishments.

Artist's insights

1 Purchase colorful slide mounts through a scrapbook supplier.

2 Unearth old aluminum mounts from an attic, flea market, or antique store.

3 Insert visual images into the slim slide-mount pockets. In this case, artist Michelle Ward has used a repetitive image of a vintage clown photo, rendered in a rainbow of colors.

4 Remember to fill the slide mounts with your visual images before affixing them to the journal cover using a layer of heavy gel medium.

5 Complete the journal with a cascade of cheerful round tags, decorative fibers, plus a rainbow-colored ribbon tie.

The Small Wonders of Slide Mounts

Does size really matter? Not when it comes to using slide mounts to create countless embellishments for journal covers and pages. You will find versions of traditional slide-mount frames in various materials, ranging from rigid plastic to conventional cardboard, as well as some vintage metal variations. More than likely, everything you need to create handfuls of slide-mount embellishments is already lurking in your collage drawers. From small pieces of paper ephemera to tiny charms and found objects, as well as short lengths of ribbon or fibers—these previously overlooked remnants can provide an arsenal of collage material and can be supplemented by tiny objects discovered in floral supply stores, fascinating import markets, your local hardware store, and the office supply warehouse. An embellishment glued to the outside of an art journal or sketchbook can provide a finishing touch or announce a compelling title treatment. On the inside pages of a journal, small openings can provide a series of windows and frames to hold tightly cropped images or rescued wisps of text or poetry. Think of an empty slide-mount frame as an instant viewfinder for discovering small wonders and big creative possibilities. Sarah Fishburn, Lisa Hoffman, Monica Riffe, and Michelle Ward took on the challenge of creating handfuls of slide-mount embellishments and found that the biggest challenge was knowing when to stop.

Slide-Mount Artwork

ARTIST MICHELLE WARD

1. Zero in on small, choice areas of gift wrap to create a miniature monument to a favorite designer or architect. Use small pieces of maps, blueprints, architectural diagrams, and navigational charts to decorate slide mounts. Use a small transparency to provide the see-through central element.

2. It's a gift! Michelle has a proven knack for finding four-leafed clovers. Use slide-mount frames to preserve and present such lucky finds. A purchase-date stamp allows you to catalogue each treasure. Apply decorative gift wrap to the outer frame to complete the look.

3. Forever female. Go through your collage drawer and find small, compelling segments of archival images. In this case, a classic Botticelli goddess tucks easily into the central opening of a slide-mount frame, which has been coated with gesso and given several coats of acrylic paints (including metallics) and a final stamping with a permanent inkpad.

4. Bee-fitting. Use small remnants from discarded costume jewelry, as well as purchased charms and decorative metal trimmings, as perfect dimensional elements to glue to a slide-mount frame. Overstamp the painted frame with a honeycomb image, and insert metal eyelets into the corners.

5. The simple pleasures: brown-paper packages tied up with string. If string, tags, and humble brown paper are some of your favorite things, you will find endless ways of using these household items for your decorative slide-mount frames. Also consider using artsy fibers, glossy buttonhole twists, or rickrack to wind around the slide-mount frames for a tactile look.

6. Fill the central portion of the slide mount with a stamped image of a door-frame with a stamped face entering the scene. Give the outer area various washes of acrylics, colored-pencil markings, and a stamped imprint with permanent ink.

7. Imprint a rubber stamp on colored cardstock, and enhance the image with gel markers to use as the central element. Use the same stamp to imprint the cardboard slide-mount frame. Additional coats of acrylic paint add to the densely colored effect.

8. A heart takes flight, thanks to carefully edited collage elements. Collage antique sheet music and script-patterned gift wrap to the outer frame. Insert a small, lightweight stone heart, flanked by tiny metallic wings, into the center opening, and glue it securely into place. A small scrap of a dictionary entry provides the comforting message.

9. Whether or not you won the raffle, you can use the saved ticket to create a fun and easy collage. Insert the colorful ticket into the center opening, and rubber-stamp the slide-mount frame. Some slide-mounts frames come with small metal strips that slide on and off. Use these strips as a finishing touch.

10. Your experiments with paper casting or working with Sculpey or Fimo can find a suitable home on a slide-mount frame. Use remnants of larger works-in-progress in the small, confined area of a slide-mount frame. These items can have visual punch with the addition of an outer frame of corrugated cardstock and stamped text.

1}
Create a black-on-black air of mystery. A reduced-size copy of a favorite bird print provided the perfect centerpiece for a cardboard slide-mount frame coated in black gesso. A small bird feather is the only other element needed to complete the story.

2}
A vintage typewriter was used to create the title, "Your Heart's Flight." Artist Lisa Hoffman imprinted a small, winged heart stamp onto a recycled cardboard slide-mount frame. A crowning element of tiny twigs and a soft, fabric leaf glued to the back of the frame appears above the composition.

3}
The next time you are splatter-painting with acrylics, lay out some cardboard slide-mount frames and allow them to catch the random splashes of color. In this example, a first coating of yellow acrylic was splatter-painted with black. After the artist inserted a small collage element in the frame opening, she wrapped the whole element in a grid of craft wire. The wire could also be used for attaching other small embellishments, such as charms.

4}
The artist glued patterned tissue paper to the cardboard slide-mount frame. A collage element from a travel brochure completes the composition.

Slide-Mount Artwork }

ARTIST LISA HOFFMAN

5}
Household products, such as joint compound, provide interesting results when used to create texture. In this case, the artist painted a light coat of metallic acrylic paint over the dried joint compound to create a golden, adobe effect. The miniature nature collage within the frame echoes the theme of the tactile surface.

6}
Affix small bits of minerals and colored rocks using household glue. The mini-mosaic effect of the rows of colored stones against the black gesso background of the slide-mount frame provides the perfect surround for a photo of statuary.

7}
Open up for a larger writing surface and include an entire poem on one slide-mount frame. Carefully pry open the frame, and write or draw on the entire surface, taking advantage of two frame openings to feature a continuous piece of artwork or two related images. In this case, Our Lady of Guadalupe appears in the openings, accompanied by a poem by Pablo Neruda. Consider applying a series of favorite poems to the pages of your travel journal, and you will have inspired reading close at hand, wherever you go.

8}
The artist painted a cardboard slide-mount frame in soft pastel colors and then wrapped the unit in a combination of narrow ribbon and rusted wire. She glued tiny seed pearls onto the frame and positioned a tightly cropped rubber-stamp image so that it seems to peer out.

9}
The smooth cardboard surface of a slide-mount frame provides a suitable surface for doing a toner transfer. The blurred image of the butterfly contrasts with the well-defined eye, surrounded by a soft fringe of frayed black fabric, in the center of the piece.

10}
The soft, tropical hues of this slide-mount frame echo the colors of the creature's image. The frame seems to provide the small home for the paper occupant.

11}
A single word, hammered into a small, copper tag, says it all. The artist added the metal embellishment to a rusted heart shape and centered a small piece of shimmering oxidized copper mesh over the painted slide-mount frame.

12}
Nothing could be simpler—The artist glued metallic foil paper to the slide-mount frame and used a pointed tool to inscribe expressive marks and letters. She reduced a dramatic black-and-white photo and inserted it inside.

13}
Mexican loteria cards make great collage elements, for both the pictorial icon and the typography. The dramatic slice of moon, tucked inside a black-gessoed slide-mount frame and simple lines drawn with a silver marking pen complete the story. Take your favorite deck of antique cards to the copy center, and create some miniature prints of your own.

14}.
A soft-hued, painted background surrounds an antique nature print. The artist added a tactile touch by carefully gluing tiny seashells on the slide-mount frame, with a small wisp of beige burlap forming the central element.

15}
The artist harvested a small, expressive face from an archival book and artfully combined it with cork-textured paper glued to the slide-mount frame, along with small, tender twigs wrapped in flexible strands of duct tape ribbon.

16}
A small sketch from your notebook can come to life when surrounded by a dramatic, black-painted slide-mount frame and a tiny feather.

17}
The small rubber stamps in your collection will work overtime when you create slide-mount frames. For this frame, two quick imprints of stamps on a painted background were given a quick shower with a plant mister.

18}
Add melted wax as a final coat, adding a textural finish and a rich coloration. Inside this slide-mount frame, a vintage advertising couple provides assurances, and expressive marks made with a fine-tipped marker seems to seal the deal.

19}
Use slide-mount frames containing small wisps of collage elements as narrative elements on a cover or page. Notice how the black-bordered frames on this page could be gathered to provide the visuals for a story. The piece takes its simple beauty from a well-chosen collage element plus a small, colorful rose sticker.

Your
Heart's
Flight

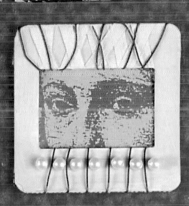

I DO NOT LOVE YOU AS IF
YOU WERE SALT ROSE, OR
TOPAZ, OR THE ARROWS
OF CARNATIONS THE FIRE
SHOOTS OFF.

I LOVE YOU AS THE PLANT THAT NEVER
BLOOMS, BUT CARRIES IN ITSELF THE
LIGHT OF HIDDEN FLOWERS...
THANKS TO YOUR LOVE, A CERTAIN
SOLID FRAGRANCE, RISEN FROM
THE EARTH, LIVES DARKLY
IN MY BODY... I LOVE YOU WITHOUT
KNOWING HOW, OR WHEN, OR
FROM WHERE. I LOVE YOU STRAIGHT
FORWARDLY, WITHOUT COMPLEXITIES
OR PRIDE; SO I LOVE YOU BECAUSE

I KNOW NO OTHER WAY

PEACE

LIGHT

LA LUNA

BEAUTY

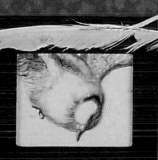

DREAM

YUP

1}
Try "sketching" with lightweight wire. Wire is available in many colors and weights and is easily bent into fascinating shapes (and even letters) that you can adhere to cardboard slide-mount frames. Use small dots of glue to hold them into place, or sew the top of the motif into place and allow the rest to dangle. Smudged pastels and a little stamping complete the embellished frame and insert.

2}
Coat the outer slide-mount frame with a thick coat of gesso. Then, brush on washes of acrylic paints, wiping away the excess to give a mottled effect. A tiny decorative border of diamond-patterned paper surrounds a small purchased sticker that was applied to a piece of gift wrap.

3}
Toss a handful of sawdust onto a slide-mount frame covered in gesso. When dry, you will have a distinctive surface upon which to build, perhaps by adding small strips of die-cut cardboard.

4}
After this recycled-cardboard slide-mount was imprinted with a textured rubber stamp, a Zenlike insert was salvaged from the artist's sketchbook. Marginal notations take on grand possibilities when presented in slide-mount frames

Slide-Mount Artwork
ARTIST MONICA RIFFE

5}
You can find small strips of numerals on packaging, dry-cleaning tags, and photo-processing envelopes. Use these numbers as subtle collage elements, combining them with functional rubber stamps normally used for dating and labeling products. A small piece of imprinted, clear plastic creates a white-on-white appearance.

6}
Try applying multiple coats of dark acrylic paint to a cardboard slide-mount frame. Then wipe down the frame between coats to create a leatherlike appearance. Use small copper brads around the central opening. Imprint a rubber stamp image, and add light sponging around the motif.

7}
A decorative sticker of a seashell affixed to a small square of burlap provides the central motif. Use pastels to decorate the outer slide-mount frame, building up multiple layers of colors, and then wind matte-finish household wire around the frame to complete the look of nautical rusticity.

8}
Add small strips of decorative cardboard to the slide-mount frame for a more dimensional look. Sometimes the reverse sides of old game cards or cardboard boxes have tiny motifs of patterning or plaid. The artist applied a color-coordinated sticker as a central element and used gel pens to mark the background.

9}
You can use wire to make small, expressive, miniature sculptures. Try doing a series of hands in various positions. The artist applied an ad from a vintage magazine collage-style to the outer slide-mount frame and created the paper insert using a blow pen and star-shaped stencils.

10}
Hand-color reduced-size photo-copies of clip art with Prismacolor pencils or gel pens, and center the art in a white cardboard slide-mount frame imprinted with markings from a pen, pencil, or marker.

11}
The torn edges from small notebooks can make an effective and interesting border design. Glue small segments to the surface and overpaint with metallic paints. Miniature travel ephemera provide the central element, framing a small-but-not-forgotten souvenir.

12}
Glue small pieces of window screen (perhaps a remnant from a repair project?) to cardboard slide-mount frames using clear house-hold glue. Waxed paper and a heavy book help to affix the screening overnight. A small rose-themed postage stamp makes the perfect centerpiece.

13}
The artist inserted a distinctive thumbprint as the central element. With the addition of small numerals and torn collage elements, this piece proves that less is more. Try a series of these, for all 10 fingers.

14}
The applied fabric leaf has the coloring of weathered copper, whereas the cardboard slide-mount frame is wound with shiny metal-foil tape. A small piece of floral-patterned paper completes the inner frame.

15}
Remember a child's game of jacks and dresses with Peter Pan collars? This slide-mount frame contains patterned paper, a single collaged word, and an insert from an old-fashioned catalog, which together tell a nostalgic story.

16}
A textured coat of gesso and rub-bings of various acrylic paints create a backdrop for a small edging of white cheesecloth. The small abstract print is an almost-overlooked scribble from a watercolor sketchbook.

17}
A rainbow of desert-pastel chalks, applied over adobe-textured gesso, makes a fitting frame to surround a small photocopied print of Our Lady of Guadalupe.

18}
Insert transparencies of vintage travel ephemera into cardboard slide-mount frames, and add color with gel pens or acrylic paints. This frame was scrubbed with a makeup sponge, which resulted in an uneven coat of color. The light-weight, rusted wire gives a dimensional aspect to the completed frame.

19}
The artist achieved this muted composition by applying loose-leaf paper reinforcements to a painted cardboard slide-mount frame. The central element is a small swatch of cheesecloth adhered to a piece of corrugated cardboard. Under most circumstances, all of these elements might be considered throwaways, but in this instance, they join forces to create a quiet and fascinating composition.

20}
Use a soft pencil to create a rubbing of a textured object. In this project, the text in the image is tightly cropped and adds a sense of mystery to the central element. The artist decorated the outer slide-mount frame with a coat of acrylic paint and markings made with oil pastels.

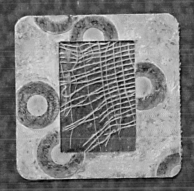

Slide-Mount Artwork

ARTIST SARAH FISHBURN

1} Decorate the cardboard slide-mount frame by sponging it with acrylic paints. Add random burnished-down lettering. Insert a reduced-sized photo into the slide interior.

2} Make miniature color prints from existing art journals at your copy center. Adhere sections of these color prints to the slide-mount frame, and insert small collages of these prints into the interior section, along with a small transit ticket. You can insert small, decorative brads through the cardboard for a final accent.

3} Adhere small swatches of text from dictionaries to the outer frame. Add imprinted metal strips to provide additional text. A small charm can underscore the message of "my lucky star." Tuck a small favorite vintage photo inside the frame to complete the narrative.

4} Paint the outer slide-mount frame with two shades of metallic acrylic paint, and then use a rubber stamp and black permanent ink. Slip a small scrap of a previous journal page into the frame opening.

5} Reduce travel brochures and advertisements on a color copier to make fascinating miniature prints. Crop some images to focus on the colors, and use these cropped images on both the outer frame and the insert. You can add small, metal brads as accents.

6} Give your rubber stamps a new look—imprint them on painted slide-mount frames. Overpaint a text stamp image to mute it, providing a background for small, golden charms. Try highlighting a collaged childhood photo in the central opening.

7} Use strips of black drafting tape to define a white cardboard slide-mount frame. Imprinted metal lettering strips (also in black and white) and silver eyelets complete the graphic look. Insert a vintage collage print for a touch of soft color.

8} Add miniature brads and small bows of buttonhole twist to a painted slide-mount frame to underscore a well-loved photo of a young girl. Paint small motifs, such as a heart, with a tiny brush, or use purchased stickers to add details.

9} Use colored pencils on a white cardboard slide-mount frame, and then imprint the frame with a text-themed rubber stamp. Adhere tiny wisps of type from previous journal pages using mat medium, and affix small, metallic jewelry with glue or stitching. A brightly colored transparency of a vintage ad provides a fun insert for the inner frame.

10} Antique ephemera, such as transit tickets, theater-ticket stubs, and train schedules, can add a perfect touch to a slide-mount frame. Use strips of black tape to bisect the elements and add visual punch. Insert black metal brads, and add reduced-size journal prints to complete the inner frame.

11} By isolating offbeat segments of larger collages, you can get more mileage from a work of art. Use tightly cropped collage sections to create curious graphic compositions, both inside and outside the frame. A colorful brad adds punch and textural interest.

12} Adhere softly hued gift wrap to the slide-mount frame, and continue the mood with tiny straw flowers, glued in place. Tuck a colorful transparency of a vintage maiden inside the opening to support the ethereal theme.

13} Try writing on the slide-mount frame with gel pens or soft pencils. Enhance your miniature journal entry with a layer of tightly woven tulle or netting, adhered with mat medium and tacked into place by four jewel-like brads. A reduced-size favorite photo completes the story.

14} Some slide-mount frames, made from recycled cardboard, are gray or brown. Enhance the background color with stenciling or airbrushing, as well as stamp imprints with permanent ink. Use small buttons as embellishments, and imprint a tiny childhood photo with evocative words.

15} Use a floral-themed rubber stamp to imprint the background of a white cardboard slide-mount frame. Add a second stamping of text or geometric design in a darker ink. Insert a wisp of paper or other item to support the mood of the frame.

16} Start collecting smaller-than-small objects to affix to your slide-mount frames. Notice how these iridescent buttons create a jewel-like touch when sewn through the cardboard and secured on the back with knots of thread. Search for small collage elements that coordinate with your color scheme, such as this tiny Art Nouveau poster.

17} Collected ephemera, such as shipping forms, diplomas, or ledger pages, become fascinating, reduced-size documents, ready to adhere to slide-mount frames. Star stickers add a metallic flash to the muted background. Photocopy text onto transparencies and slip them into the frame, along with a collage scrap.

18} After giving the slide-mount frame several coats of acrylic paint (including metallics), stamp it with more than one rubber stamp, building up layers of images and color. Postage stamps, which are designed to pack visual punch into a small area, make ideal inserts. Include fascinating postal cancellations, too.

19} Small-patterned fabric is ideal for slide-mount frames. You can stitch it right through the cardboard. Use pinking shears to trim the edges before you affix it, and remember that basting, decorative stitching, and even safety pins continue the look of tiny textile collages. A warm-hued color transparency completes the look of a small fabric decorative frame.

20} After adhering a collage print to the cardboard frame, use small metallic brads to stud the surface. Crop colorful sections of exotic postage stamps, isolating interesting segments in the inner frame of the slide mount. Consider doing a whole series based on a grouping of themed postage stamps.

The artist describes a color-drenched trip to the fabric store, as she chose the needed materials to make this soft-sided art journal—"Ah, sweet color! Lilac, raspberry, and plum, and an outspoken, zingy green print and some sassy green ribbon and purple fringe."

Soft-Sided Journal

ARTIST LINN C. JACOBS

Fabric-covered artist's journal with adornments

Artist's insight

Plan ahead. Otherwise your stitching to attach beads, charms, and embellishments will be seen on the "right" side of your journal.

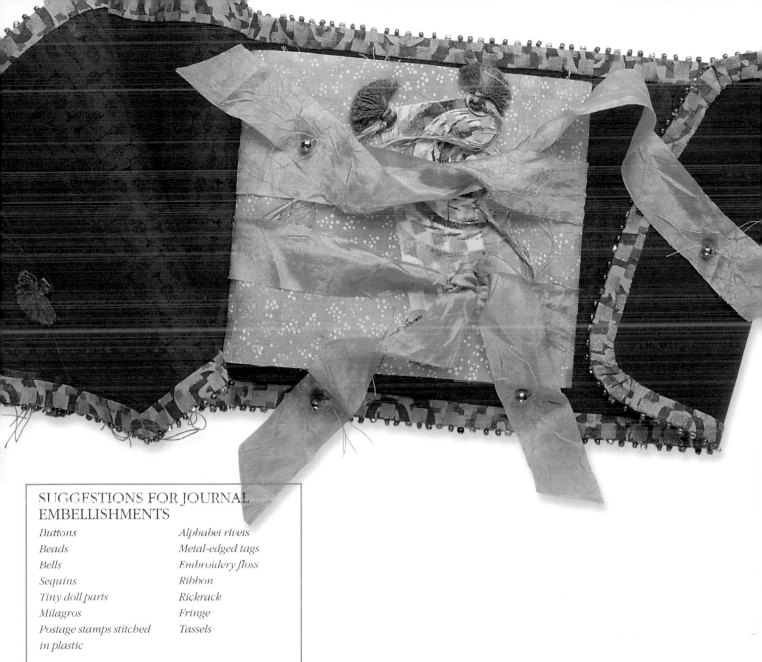

SUGGESTIONS FOR JOURNAL EMBELLISHMENTS

Buttons

Beads

Bells

Sequins

Tiny doll parts

Milagros

Postage stamps stitched in plastic

Alphabet rivets

Metal-edged tags

Embroidery floss

Ribbon

Rickrack

Fringe

Tassels

HOW TO MAKE A FABRIC-COVERED JOURNAL

1. Create the inner journal, using watercolor paper for the signatures. Green fabric, with some additional stencilling using fabric paint, forms the covers of the journal. This finished element determines the measurements and details for the wraparound fabric cover. Adding 2" (5.1cm) to the width of the journal, calculate the length plus enough for a generous-sized flap.

2. Both the cover fabric (lilac) and the lining (raspberry) were cut to the same size and ironed together using fusible interfacing.

3. The outer edges were bound with bias binding tape that had been stencilled with fabric paints. Small, colorful seed beads were also stitched to the center fold of the bias tape, before it was hand-stitched into place, all along the edges of the lilac cover.

4. Attach the inner journal to the outer cover, including the green fabric ties embellished with tiny brass bells. Stitch through all the layers, securing the threads on the outside and hiding the threads with an embellishments of fringe, glass beads, and decorative fibers.

5. Secure the outermost ties of purple grosgrain ribbon.

Out of the kitchen, and into the studio. Create a celestial and glistening journal cover using heavy-duty aluminum foil. This successful experiment in appropriating household goods for glowing results began with a length of heavy-duty aluminum foil folded around a rigid sheet of smooth cardboard.

1. Use various burnishing tools to create lines and patterns on the surface. Use care, so as not to tear the foil. (The artist prefers Dr. Martin's acrylic inks to add the luminous colors.)

2. Once you are happy with the pattern and colors, use a blow dryer to set the piece. Then adhere it to a purchased journal, using Perfect Paper Adhesive (PPA). A final layer of PPA protects the cover from wear.

3. Keep an eye out for found objects with interesting surfaces and patterns, such as discarded costume jewelry, bottle caps, and fragments of metallic castoffs. These finds can be pressed into action to create medallions for book covers, using Fimo or Sculpey.

The wonders of aluminum foil

Journal #29

ARTIST BILLYE MIRAGLIA

Artist's insight

If you change your mind about your ink designs, you can wipe the surface smooth with ammonia and start over.

Create an index-card journal

}Artfest Journal

ARTIST MONICA RIFFE

One of the hundreds of wisps of found typography in this index-card journal reads, "The Traveler's Fun Book." This full-to-bursting, purse-size journal started out as a plain-vanilla, spiral-bound book of index cards. The artist tucked this book into her travel bag as she headed off to a creativity retreat with other paper artists. She used any spare moment to glue, paste, stitch, and staple random paper souvenirs and memory fodder into her book. A look inside reveals various trades from other artists, classroom notations, on-the-spot poetry, travel notes and jottings, postage stamps, stickers, and instant photos taken at the retreat. The resultant book, telescoping out into a half-circle of visual treats and remembrances, is a vivid example of how new experiences can be documented, saved, and savored.

Two doll-like sentries guard the inner pages of the artist's engaging and colorful fabric-covered journal.

Funky Fabric-Covered Journal

ARTIST TEESHA MOORE

} *Creating a mixed-media art journal*

This project is a natural for anyone who wants to take an experimental and spontaneous approach to quilting and sewing, without any of the worries about accurate measuring or specific equipment, such as a sewing machine. The imperfect, handmade look of the journal cover is the key to its charm—the secret ingredient that makes it easy to do.

As you become more comfortable with this quilting technique, you may want to expand your horizons to other projects, such as quilts, wall hangings, banners, or purses. Consider other fabric choices such as velvet, satin, or silk to create a different look.

SUGGESTED MATERIALS

Cotton fabrics

Fabric transfers on muslin (See pages 28–29 for more information on transfers of all kinds.)

Regular sewing needles for straight stitching

Crewel needles for the decorative stitching

Cotton thread

DMC pearl cotton thread, #5

Poly-fil stuffing to fill the various segments, before quilting

Buttons

Charms

HOW TO MAKE A FUNKY FABRIC-COVERED JOURNAL

1. Make a paper pattern of your proposed journal cover.

2. Create the individual fabric segments by cutting two layers of different fabrics, allowing an additional ⅜" (1 cm) for seam allowances. (If you plan to add fabric transfers, now is the time to hand-sew them into place.)

3. Sew the segments, right sides together, along three sides, using a straight stitch. Turn the piece right-side-out, and fill the "pillow" with enough Poly-fil to create a 1"-thick (2,5 cm-thick) section. Once you have evenly distributed the Poly-fil, hand-stitch closed the open end of the pillow. Repeat this procedure for all the segments of your project.

4. Using pearl cotton, create a whipstitch around all edges of each fabric pillow. Begin quilting each pillow, making small, random stitches through the pillow from front to back. You may want to add stitching to enhance the fabric transfers or add buttons, beads, or French knots. Use a variety of colored threads for a handmade look.

5. Once you have quilted and embellished the segments, use the same thread and whipstitch technique to connect them. If you plan to add a button and buttonhole, be sure to not add quilting to that area.

6. Stitch the signatures of your journal into the fabric cover, using the same needle and thread that you used for quilting. For the featured journal, the artist created a format of interlocking signatures of pages, plus long and short folds that reveal the different journal entries throughout. She glued decorative braid in various widths to the inside pages to continue the funky fabric theme of the cover.

Virginia Woolf frequently referred to her journal as a "capacious hold-all," an unruly desk that contained all her secrets, truths, proclamations, and wonderings.

Make your art journal a more personal document by including the miscellanea of your daily life on your pages. If you are an inveterate collector, there is no reason to not extend that habit to your art journal. As you become more aware of tricks and techniques for attaching fond and found objects to your pages, your journal will become a more tactile and revealing volume. Gluing objects onto a page is always an option, but you can use additional techniques and products to make the art of attachment into a creative adventure. Artist Michelle Ward invites us to consider the possibilities.

Attachment techniques

ARTIST MICHELLE WARD

1}
Attach a brass bezel with acrylic dome (Renaissance Art Stamps) using gel medium. Collage by Heather Foti. Attach a brass label plate with black miniature brads.

2}
Mount a stamped face (Acey Deucy Rubber Stamps) under acetate, and mount a brass rim (Fancifuls, Inc.) with black miniature brads on painted paper. Attach with red photo corners.

3}
Use self-adhesive index tabs, inserted with patterned paper.

If your journal has a spiral binding, you have a built-in starting point for making creative attachments. Start building a collection of ribbons, decorative threads, waxed linen, fibers, and craft wire in various colors, plus metallics, twine, and leather to use as "ties" for various visual add-ons, for your pages. Michelle Ward provides two suggestions:

4}
Mount a brass starfish charm with wire wrap and beads over amber mica. Attach with bronze eyelets over brass washers.

5}
Attach a brass woman charm (Renaissance Art Stamps) using gel fixative, and brush with Pearl-Ex. Attach a brass nameplate, collaged with a stamped word, using colored eyelets.

6}
Create a tab by stringing beads on wire, and loop and wrap it through eyelets. Sew an acorn charm on under ribbon.

Left
Paint and stamp a coin envelope, and trim it to size. Attach decorative metal eyelets at the edge. Loop colored raffia through the spiral binding and eyelet holes, and tie it off and trim. Envelopes can hold keepsakes, written journal passages, or favorite quotations or lyrics.

7}
Tie a brass "Secrets" charm (Stampers Anonymous) through punched holes. Attach a metal-edged circular tag with a large metal eyelet and a metal-rimmed vellum tag using an eyelet.

8}
Create a tab using the top of a manila shipping tag, and attach it with colored fasteners. String with decorative fibers.

Right
Edge transparencies or colored acetate with copper tape. Punch holes, and finish them off with copper eyelets. Loop copper wire through the spiral binding and eyelets, and then wrap it tightly and trim. Add text to the copper tape using an inscribing tool.

9}
Attach an embellished coin envelope (remove the flap, and use a circle punch to reveal the inserted tag) with miniature brads. Add a printed ribbon (Stampers Anonymous).

10}
Trim and mount a stamped image of a window over text using miniature brads.

11}
Use a raffle ticket, glued to edge of page, as a tab. Paint acrylic die-cut letters (Coffee Break Designs) on the back, and attach it with gel medium.

Avoiding the pain and suffering of being caught without a journal handy, the artist has used a discarded aspirin tin to create a palm-size, 1½" x 2" (3.8cm x 5.1cm) book.

For All Time

ARTIST TRACY V. MOORE

Handmade journal

Only a large imagination would spot the creative potential of such a small throwaway, plus find a manageable way of turning tin into treasure. After taking the tin apart, the artist used his handy Dremel tool to grind the existing paint from the surface and introduced a distressed, textured surface. He used Rub n Buff to add darkened highlights.

He placed embellishments, including a discarded watch face and strips of brass with hammered words, inside the tin cover and added ultra-thick embossing powder. He used a heat gun to achieve the finished hardened surface. The covers and signatures of hot-press watercolor paper are bound together with a coptic stitch.

JOURNALING QUICK TIPS

1. Small is beautiful. Train your eye to discern the creative possibilities of tiny boxes and small, throwaway packaging. You can use the previous techniques to create a journal embellishment, using half of an aspirin tin as a shrine to feature small items, such as milagros, coins, and jewelry.

2. Create a fun series of aspirin-tin journals using found house numerals from a metal salvage yard in a series of covers. Once you begin to approach artwork from the perspective of a series, the possibilities are endless.

This handmade journal gives new meaning to the phrase "talking shop."

Book of Dreams

ARTIST TRACY V. MOORE

}

Handmade journal

Using tricks and tools in his woodshop work-room, the artist has created an engaging, hand-made journal, ready to receive dreams and sketches for future projects. The small size, 2" x 3" (5.1cm x 7.6cm), allows this sturdy book to be slipped into a carryall bag—or displayed on a sideboard with a collection of other wooden and brass objects. Either way, the look is handsome and artful. The artist made the front and back covers of 22-gauge nickel silver, cut with tin snips. He created the protruding spheres using a small ball peen hammer and a block. The artist's woodshop is equipped with alphabet stamping sets in several sizes. He hammered brass strips with the book title and used a rub-on metallic glaze to darken and highlight the letters. He attached the word strips to the cover using pin rivets. He bound signatures of hot-press watercolor paper to the leather spine and attached the metal cover with waxed polyester binding line through holes drilled with a miniature drill.

JOURNALING QUICK TIPS

If your expertise does not extend to the woodshop, you can still add a handcrafted look to a purchased journal.

1. Use contact cement to attach edgings or corners of leather or suede to a journal.

2. Use sturdy leather thongs or rugged shoelaces for wrap-around closures.

3. Attach embellishments with brass eyelets, metal brads, and craft wire.

4. Use faux-finishing paint effects to create the look of exotic woods, such as ebony, cocobola wood, or African rosewood.

An endless variety of handmade exotic papers sets the tone for a continual parade of journaling "prompts" as the artist celebrates her love of paper and joy of experimentation.

From wispy, fly-away sheets of see-through tissue paper to vivid and multipatterned paste papers, this beautiful handmade book proves that more is more. Each page presents a different and unique challenge, unlike a conventional purchased journal full of white pages. Every time this book falls open, a new and exciting opportunity to respond to the colors, patterns, and textures awaits.

ARTIST **ALBIE SMITH**

The Book of Plenty

} *Mixed-media journal containing multiple papers*

PAPER SAMPLER

From top to bottom:

Office envelope with button-and-tie closure

Animal-print gift wrap

Vintage correspondence

A selection of paste papers

Watercolor paper

Hand-marbleized imported paper

Vintage music sheet

Rusted-brown wrapping paper

Stitched Thai paper

Corrugated stock

Metallic copper paper

Foreign newspaper

Handmade seaweed tissue paper

Handmade pulp coverweight stock

JOURNALING QUICK TIP

Most large commercial copy centers offer binding services. Take a stack of your favorite collected papers and ask them to create a spiral binding and—voila!—you'll have a ready-to-use journal. Include various textures, colors, weights, and sizes of paper. Never be at a loss for ideas or impulses—each unique journal page provides a different prompt.

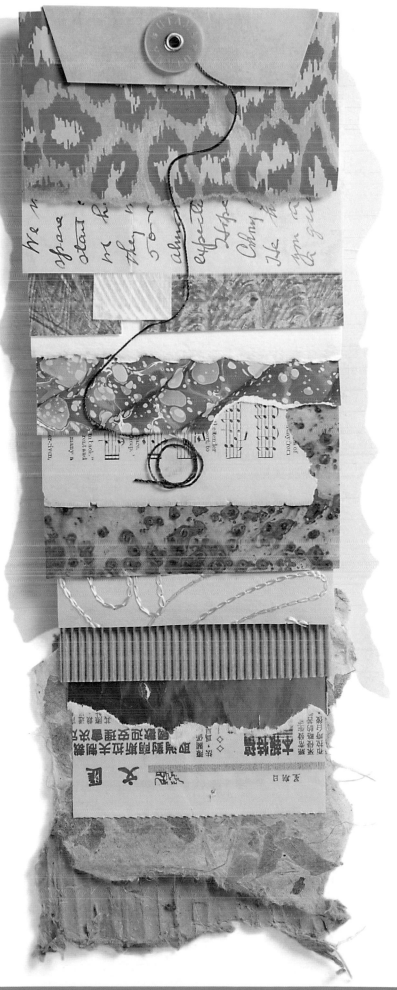

3

True
Fiction

Adding text to pages

"To write is to descend, to excavate, to go underground." Anaïs Nin

Each entry in an art journal reflects a moment in time. Although some pages may depend on purely visual expressions, possibilities for adding text to pages are limitless. A strong connection exists between current day art journals and the time-honored traditions of written diaries. Think of your art journal as a place to express the entire spectrum of your world, and consider whether the use of language would make that expression more real and vital. As with the entire journaling process, there are no rules for adding words to your pages—but, rest assured, hundreds of fascinating ways to do it abound.

The words you add to your pages can be as mundane as a to-do list or as shattering as a personal manifesto. Either way, the time you spend committing these words to your pages is part of your personal creative journey.

In this chapter, you will learn a wide variety of ideas and techniques for integrating text, and you will begin to develop your own sense of how to make your pages more revelatory and expressive by adding words. I have discovered many different techniques and tools for placing words on a page, and I have come to realize that each journal entry may require, or perhaps even invite, a different treatment. You do not have to be a master calligrapher to create a vibrant and expressive journal page; in fact, the unique character of your own hand-writing on a page makes it significant and personal. Remember that words are a terrific jump start to creativity. If you are having trouble getting started with a page, pull out your file of favorite quotes or go to a quotation dictionary and allow these treasured words to spur your own creative process. I have always been drawn to works of art that include an element of handwriting or script. They instantly communicate something about the hand of the artist, the individual who created the work. In that same way, your placement of words on a page can further illuminate your visual pages, better reflecting your state of mind.

Within this chapter, you'll see various art materials and their possibilities. I always keep a lot of different supplies in my arsenal. However, one of my favorite techniques for adding words to a page is to use a soft #2 black pencil, writing over the surface of my pages. What could be simpler?

12 IDEAS FOR ADDING TEXT TO PAGES

1. Imprint the page with rubber-stamp alphabets.

2. Add a painterly quality by using hand-carved eraser stamps dipped into acrylic paint.

3. Provide instant expression or an air of mystery using collaged words clipped from newspapers or magazines.

4. Cover your pages in large, expressive handwriting, using a fountain pen and inks, colored Prisma pencils, markers, or gel pens.

5. Add words and passages via applied elements, such as tags or labels.

6. Incorporate into your pages hidden compartments that reveal special messages or thoughts.

7. Write on see-through elements such as vellum or transparencies.

8. Build up a surface of multiple layers of handwriting, allowing some words to float to the surface and others to descend.

9. Use press-on lettering or purchased stencils.

10. Bend wire or pipe cleaners into words, and affix them to your pages and covers.

11. Harvest words from a collection of ephemera, including sheet music, diplomas, documents, correspondence, and postcards. If you savor the look of stylish writing but do not do expert calligraphy yourself, consider collaging the curvaceous lettering found in old legal documents and ledgers onto your pages.

12. Consider using a sewing machine or hand stitching to add elements to your pages, allowing the stitching lines to provide yet another form of mark-making to the surface.

Tuck lettering and text into the multiple layers of each journal page. By avoiding clear, readable words, you can provide the impression of an overheard conversation or a poetic passage written on water.

ARTIST BRENDA MURRAY

One Woman's Journey

} *Building layers of text and color*

Artist's Insights

1 Begin a clipping file of words and phrases from offbeat sources, such as newspapers, dry-cleaning tags, and theater ticket stubs, and you will always have a compelling starting point for a journal entry.

2 Try working on sheets of watercolor paper. This will allow you to work on several pages (perhaps from differently sized journals) at once, without the usual waiting for paints to dry. Your completed pages can be bound between rigid covers, using Chicago screws.

3 Artist Brenda Murray's mantra for developing her pages is "integrate." Begin a page with a wash of acrylic paints, and then cover the surface with handwritten freestyle script. Adhere elements of torn paper, photocopied images (try the same image in several different sizes), old documents, and fragments of type, and use more washes of paints between the layers.

4 Photographs can be altered by sanding, over-painting, tearing, or adding solvents.

5 Consider applying acrylic glazes to part of the page or to the entire page, or applying metallic paints for a rich, subtle look. Additional lettering or handwriting can be added, using a fine-point pen or gel marker.

SUGGESTED MATERIALS	Watercolor paper	Pencil and eraser	Artist brushes, including very fine ones for lettering	Craft knife and self-healing cutting mat
	Chicago screws	Pens and gel markers	Makeup sponge	Waxed paper (to protect pages that are not fully dry)
	Assorted paper scraps and ephemera	Acrylic paints	Purchased or hand-carved alphabet stamps	PVA glue
		Metallic paints		

Using color (top)

To create a mood of strong contrast, consider using warm and cool colors on opposing pages. Previous layers of handwriting plus rubber-stamped words will give your pages a strong foundation as you build the surface, using blocks of color to compartmentalize thoughts and ideas. Although Brenda Murray's pages provide a strong statement about color and abstraction, the addition of recognizable collage elements like the vintage portrait pulls the viewer into the mystery, while the words *Power* and *Positive* float on the surface.

Using maps & stamps (bottom)

Ordinary roadmaps take on the extraordinary look of ancient charts, plus provide an effective way of bisecting the page and attracting the eye to the text. The pages of your art journal may be the perfect forums for exploring questions, great and small. Sometimes the answer to a dilemma will emerge on a page, as you work. A self-carved stamp of a medieval star motif was used to overprint this page, adding a strong visual exclamation point to the compositon. Small, carved stamps are easily carried in a portable journaling kit, ready to add to the pages you may do "on the run."

Experimenting (right)

The artist's personal credo about beginning a journal page is "I start." Remember that your materials suggest compositions, messages, themes, and tone. It is not important to have a firm idea of what the finished page will look like, or a master plan for specific results. This page shows several ideas for adding text, including a collaged alphabet, handwritten phrases, burnished-down lettering, and penciled inscriptions, among others. Be willing to keep working a page until it conveys the feeling you want, and remember that an unsuccessful page can be painted over or torn into pieces and used as collage fodder.

Just take a moment.
Reflect and think.
Really think. You

ABCDEFG

turn around

SHARE
THE IDEA

"A haiku per day, for two months." That was the exercise that Anne Bagby set for herself with this journal.

Haiku Journal

ARTIST ANNE BAGBY

Keeping a real-world poetry journal

She selected a compact spiral-bound journal that would slip easily into a tote bag or backpack. She used hand-carved alphabet stamps to imprint the cover with a title and used other purchased rubber stamps to decorate the background. A tangle of beaded embellishments strung on wire add an artistic touch, and the all-black painted shipping tag seems to emphasize the spare, Zenlike quality of the poetic verses inside and also allude to the "blank slate" that exists as we approach any poetry assignment. By covering the inside and outside surfaces of the book with various mark-making techniques, The artist has quickly "claimed" this book as her own personal repository for observations and awakenings, transforming a purchased journal into a revealing and personal document.

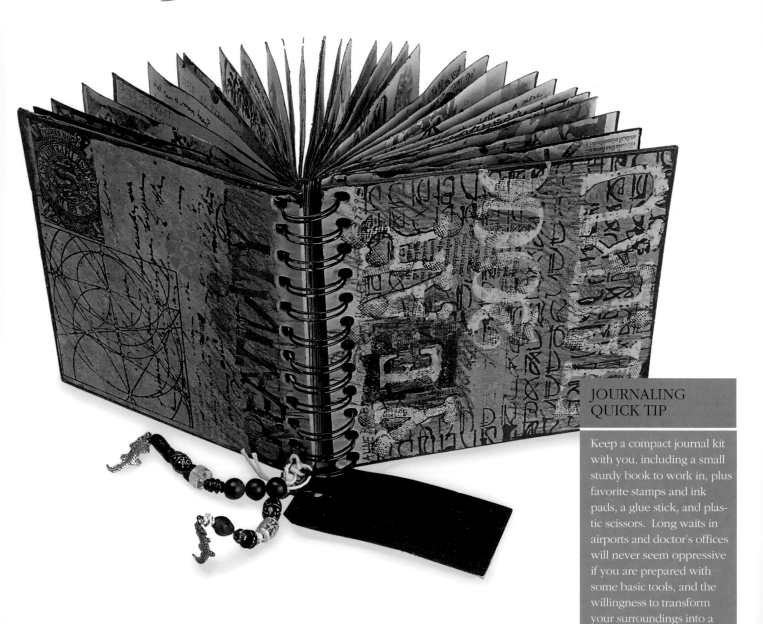

JOURNALING QUICK TIP

Keep a compact journal kit with you, including a small sturdy book to work in, plus favorite stamps and ink pads, a glue stick, and plastic scissors. Long waits in airports and doctor's offices will never seem oppressive if you are prepared with some basic tools, and the willingness to transform your surroundings into a creative respite.

Experimenting with writing implements

The artist's written notations, in both ballpoint pen and fine-tipped marker, provide a textbook example of how our own handwriting creates a strong individualistic statement on a page. In this journal spread, she has used any writing implement at hand to record the poetry of her thoughts as she worked in this traveling visual diary. Favorite quotations, overheard dialogs, and shopping lists also crowd into the book, providing evidence of the real world, side by side with experimental poetry. She has also used the book to proof her hand-carved rubber stamps, allowing these random imprints to provide the "illustrations" for her book of poems. Her willingness to keep working on a page until it is fully loaded with images has resulted in a rich tapestry-like surface of words and patterns.

Stamp carving

Anne Bagby's hand-carved stamps may remind some of the tendrilled historical designs of William Morris, although her techniques for both carving and imprinting are thoroughly contemporary.

1 To create a stamp like this one, start with a copyright-free design from a textile archive. Make a photocopy of the artwork. To transfer the image to the carving surface, coat the carving block with mat medium, place the artwork face down, burnish lightly with a soft cloth, and allow it to dry. Once dry, run the block under water to lift off the copy paper and expose the design.

2 Begin cutting away all the black areas of the design using a linoleum-block cutting tool, with various blade sizes. Alternatively, you can carve out the white areas. Create your designs in both positive and negative versions to give you more design flexibility.

3 To begin printing, apply acrylic paints to the surface using small makeup sponges, or try ink pads and markers to achieve different effects. Achieve shaded, airbrushed effects by applying multiple colors to the block for a single imprint. Create an overall layered effect by over-printing and by creating slightly offset imprints as well as by using positive and negative imprints. Use your stamps to imprint journal pages or to create one-of-a-kind papers to use in collages.

4 Here is an example of one of Anne's hand stamped papers. If you plan to use your carved stamps in a repeated pattern, be sure to mark the "top" of the design on the back surface of your printing block. Your carved designs may become the final imprint on a page that has been sponged, comb-painted, or washed with acrylics, or you may decide to imprint the page with a carved stamp and add successive layers of other techniques, for a muted appearance

Mandala
ARTIST JULIANA COLES

}

*Defining the
self with color*

Although the dictionary defines *mandala* as "a symbol representing the effort to reunify the self," Juliana Coles has redefined it as a vehicle for decoding emotions through the use of color. The entry on the left, written in ballpoint pen on handmade paper and masking tape, explores the significance and meaning of each of the colors she has chosen for her personal mandala. Starting with ultramarine blue and working through to magenta, each color is explored in visual terms as well as in written notations in her text. The vivid painting of the mandala is also inscribed with more writing, in marking pen, and given some shimmering highlights of glitter.

Letter to a stranger

}Dear Alice

ARTIST JULIANA COLES

Need a starting point for a journal page? Try describing yourself in a letter to a stranger, as this artist and workshop teacher recommends. Her own books form a startling creative library of emotions and observations. Here, she checks back in with Alice Boner, an artist who lived in Paris and India in the '20s and '30s. Alice, Alice, are you still listening? is the question, asked and answered on these pages. A sheet of vintage ledger paper becomes the letter-writing surface for this journal spread, and collage elements are also added, along with a delicate tassel from an Asian market. The "official" stampings on the edges of the pages stand in direct contrast to the written journal entry, as the artist takes stock of her world and shares her teaching experiences with Alice Boner, kindred soul. The addition of strips of masking tape to these pages is proof positive of the functional beauty of the simple things that hold us all together.

Journal cards

Have you ever gone to your drawing table, ready to work in your art journal, and found yourself devoid of ideas and creative jump starts? Sometimes it only takes an image, a word, a quotation, or a color to get started. The Journal Cards, at right, were designed to give you a handful of creative prompts, as well as to evoke your own visions and ideas. Copy the artwork onto a piece of cardstock, cut along the indicated lines, and keep your set of Journal Cards in a tin or pouch. Allow a card, selected randomly, to suggest a beginning for a page. Add to the deck with your own cards, or ask other artists to collaborate on an expanded version of this Idea Deck.

CUT AT GUIDELINES

CUT AT GUIDELINES

Invent a Symbol

Metaphor

Tell Your Story

Define Yourself

Welcome the child within

QUANTUM LEAP

RAGING COLOR

Labyrinth Dance

Memory On A Page

Embrace chaos!

Dream Arch

Ambiguity

Unedited Intensity

NARRATIVE

SUGGESTED MATERIALS

Unprimed canvas

Acrylic paints

Inexpensive brushes, various sizes

Brause pen nibs

Inks, both solid colors and pearlescent

Family memorabilia

Photo transfers

Charms, ribbons, amulets

Thread, various colors including metallic

Vintage fabric and lace

The Dress Still Hangs in the Garage Closet

Turning personal memorabilia into a collage

ARTIST LISA ENGELBRECHT

Family memorabilia, collage elements, and charms, plus the addition of beautiful, flowing calligraphy is the artist's personal formula for creating journal pages steeped in legacy and lore. This tactile page documents the engagement and marriage of the artist's mother and features transfers of photos and clippings of announcements, which create a touchable evocation of these long-ago, happy occasions. The artist works on squares of unprimed canvas, brushing on a wash of diluted acrylic inks. She then uses dip pens to write the free associations that come to mind. Photo images are borrowed from family scrapbooks and made into fabric transfers (see pages 28–29 for more information on transfers). She hand-sews these transfers onto the background using decorative stitches or sews them with a sewing machine using metallic thread. She glues or stitches collage elements, small charms, and amulets to the canvas, as well as soft wisps of gauzy ribbon. The artist's distinctive and skillful calligraphy add a master touch to these heartfelt and touchable pages. Her techniques for making tactile and unique journal entries can be adopted by nonlettering artists as well. The success of her canvas pages centers on the creative harvesting of family memorabilia, using art supplies and found objects from today to tell a vivid story about yesteryear.

JOURNALING QUICK TIPS

1. Use a sewing machine to stitch elements to paper pages.

2. Use metallic touches, in both threads and inks, to add a luminous appearance and to provide a visual link to charms and amulets.

3. If you are not a skilled calligrapher, consider adding words to your canvas via purchased rubber-stamp alphabets. Apply fabric inks to the stamps with a small makeup sponge.

4. Raid the attic. Look for old memorabilia such as gloves, handkerchiefs, odd bits of costume jewelry, varsity letters, graduation tassels, and other almost-forgotten pieces of family lore. Include these treasures in your pages, and make color copies for the rest of the family to enjoy.

"I love all things postal!"

Be inspired by a favorite artist or a great exhibit

}

Icon Post
ARTIST SUE NAN DOUGLASS

This remark from the artist might explain why she chose to create a limited edition of faux postage to commemorate a visit to a definitive Andy Warhol exhibit. After being steeped in the world of Warhol for an entire day, the artist used her skills as a letterer and expert stamp carver to create a journal page that is in sync with Warhol's well-known belief in posterized images and strong color. Using her customary carving material of choice, a Mars Staedtler Grand eraser, she created the carved portrait of Andy, plus the appropriate cancellation stamp used to imprint the final sheet of postage and make it look official. With collage elements, she changed Andy's look in each frame, while maintaining an overall strong color scheme that would make the Pop Art icon smile in appreciation. Her written journal notations, describing the day of museum-gazing, begin in the margins of the postal sheet and continue on successive pages. The next time you have been stirred by a sighting or event, use your journal pages to carry the energy forward. Don't wait for the postal authority to pay homage to a favorite artist—get out your carving tools, and begin the celebration on your own journal pages.

SUGGESTED MATERIALS

Mars Staedtler Grand eraser

Linoleum-block carving tool set

Inkpads

Solid-color decorative papers

Collage papers

Lettering pen or fine-tipped marker

Photo corners

JOURNALING QUICK TIPS

1. Carry a notebook or sketchbook to museums and galleries. Your quick notations will capture the essence of the experience and provide plenty of raw material for journal pages done later in your studio.

2. Follow your passions. The artist's lifelong fascination with postal images has become a key element in her works of art, from journal pages to collages.

3. Explore the whole range of possibilities for imprinting hand-carved stamps. Inkpads are available in nearly every color of the spectrum, as well as rainbow effects, metallics, and pearlescent shades. Overstamping in several colors, plus off register imprints, can create unexpected and interesting surprises. Don't forget that you can also apply acrylic paints to stamps, but be sure to clean the stamps afterwards.

Once again we are out of town and I find myself thinking of ideas galore. I think thru different perspectives and of course peering around. Creative people, all write my brain superactive. There are so many things I want to try but I know that when I get home these ideas will all fade and I will lose a lot of that enthusiasm. I need to find time to do fresh, new creative stuff since my business and sanity all depend on it...

Adding text while exploring color

ARTIST TEESHA MOORE

Playing with Words, Edge-to-Edge

With a trusted arsenal of favorite art supplies, the artist can turn any spare moment into an opportunity for creating more vivid journal pages. Whether working in her own studio or in a coffee house or bookstore, she always finds a way to explore ideas or save creative impulses in her books. Try to create a saturated background color that goes right to the edge of each page, and use an ever-expanding group of tools for adding text to your journal entries. The artist is constantly experimenting with different writing implements as her own techniques for creating color and pattern on a page evolves. She uses wide array of brush pens, mechanical and technical pens, gel markers, colored pencils, rubber-stamp alphabet sets, and wax crayons to create her rollicking pages. She advocates drawing lines with a brush marker and then using a writing tool to inscribe journal entries at a later time—perhaps as you wait for an iced latte. She always has several pages in different stages, ready to work on when inspiration strikes. One final word of advice: Don't forget to doodle!

ARTIST CONNIE NEWBANKS

My Goal

Allowing a page to develop and unfold

Use a journal as a place to enjoy integrating the art disciplines you have learned, whether they be collage, lettering, painting, drawing, or stamping. To avoid being confronted by stark, white pages of watercolor paper, the artist favors covering her pages with color, using pastel chalks, watercolor washes, or acrylic paints. The featured pages were painted with Jacquard textile mediums, applied with a wet sponge. Once the pigment is on the page, she adds words and phrases, working around the strong collage elements in each composition, with shades of watercolor crayons. The exciting color base invites the various sizes and styles of lettering, all executed with different tools.

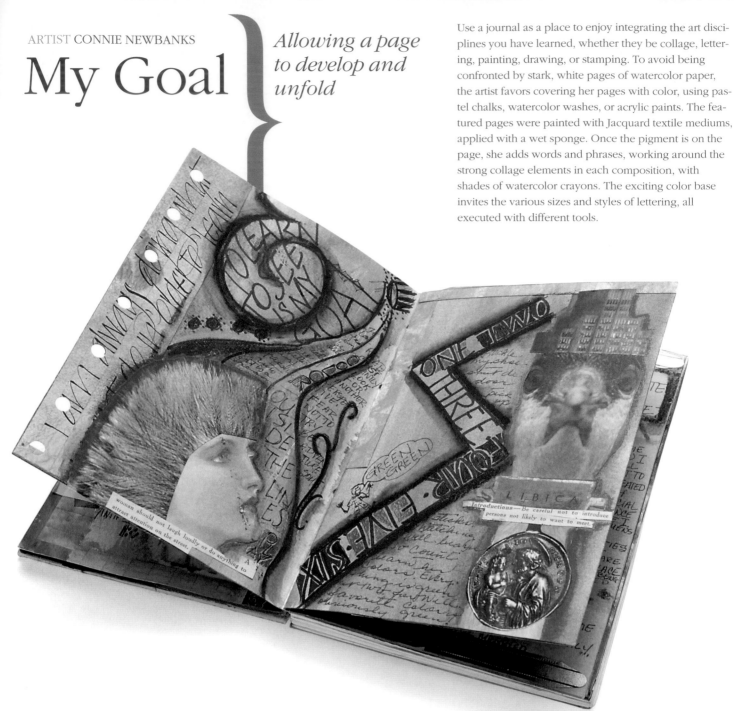

Artist's insights

1 Create a collage file of images that fascinate you. Make these appropriated images your own by reinventing them. Notice how this artist has combined a woman's profile with sheaves of wheat.

2 Experiment with strong color. If a page ends up too vibrant, apply a wash of darker color to darken the composition.

3 Keep tools accessible and attractively arranged. Create a still life with your various writing implements and brushes. Find interesting containers for everyday art supplies, and change the arrangement frequently to please your eye. Stoneware jugs and crocks, various imported coffee cans, clay garden pots and urns, or colorful vintage kitchenware are all possibilities.

4 If a journal page is not turning out to your satisfaction, apply gesso over the top of everything and start over.

SUGGESTED MATERIALS

Pens, markers, and writing implements

Textile mediums

Makeup sponges

Watercolor crayons

Collage elements

*Adding hand-
stamped text
and poetry*

}

ARTIST ROBIN ATKINS

Prayer

JOURNALING QUICK TIPS

1. Begin a poetry journal in a blank book. Include your favorites by other poets, and also use the book for your own experimentations with poetry, haiku, or stream-of-consciousness jottings.

2. Before you begin stamping your journal page, you may find it useful to do a trial run by imprinting the words of your poem on a piece of paper to find the correct spacing for a pleasing composition. Keep in mind that you can overpaint, comb-paint, or sponge these trial stampings with acrylic paints and keep them in your collage file for another use.

The time and care that it takes to hand-stamp a poem using a rubber-stamp alphabet allows you to regard each word of the poem and commit it to memory, as well as to present it on a meaningful journal page. Here, the artist has created a hand-bound book to hold a poem that she created at an art retreat. This book features an accordion style fold out of water-color paper, and each page is a delight to view and touch, thanks to tactile elements such as silk swatches, metallic fibers, tiny shells glued into place, and rough-surfaced, handmade paste papers. Begin a collection of various-sized rubber-stamp alphabets so that you will always be ready to imprint your pages with instant typography. Combine the different sizes of type and different colors of ink, or mix the type fonts for an adventurous ransom-note look. In this case, the consistent size and color of the stamp imprints reflect the dignity and insight of her poetry, allowing her to self-publish her writing exercise, as well as embellish the pages with heartfelt collages that add color and texture to the overall composition. Notice how personal and intimate the pages look, even though handwriting is not included.

SUGGESTED MATERIALS

Watercolor paper, scored and folded

Inkpads in various colors

Fabric swatches

Fibers

Small shells and beads

Paste papers

Joss paper

GLUE, SHOW ME HOW TO BIND MY HEART TO ANOTHER AND HOLD ITSELF THERE, LONG AND FIRM. PAPER, BRING HANDMADE CARE TO MORE THAN MY ART. BRING YOUR PRIDE TO MY MOST ROUTINE ACTS.

Pages from Journal #32

ARTIST BILLYE MIRAGLIA

Seek inspiration from location

Use a journal entry to assume the colors and textures of a favorite travel location. In this project, the artist brought the sunlight and deep expressive colors of Italy into her daily chronicles. She uses purchased, spiral-bound watercolor journals, preparing the pages with washes of acrylic paints. In a modern-day version of illuminated manuscripts, she gathers collage materials that seem to marry with her daily writings, as well as favorite saved quotations. She added the visual elements with mat medium and blended them into the background with paints. The handwriting in black fine-tipped marker, which floats on top of the watery colorful background, allows both the words and the images to share center stage.

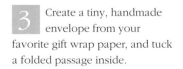

Artist's insights

1 Add smaller-than-small envelopes to journal pages to hold paper treasures.

2 Create a special hiding place for a journal entry or perhaps a favorite quotation or poem.

3 Create a tiny, handmade envelope from your favorite gift wrap paper, and tuck a folded passage inside.

4 Tuck a soft feather or a sprig of lavender into the envelope for an added grace note. Each time you remove the contents from its special place, you will be reminded of the innately private and secret nature of journals and diaries.

Presenting a dimensional page

A Gentle Rapping at the Door of My Heart

ARTIST LINN C. JACOBS

The artist has invented several techniques for presenting personal words and inscribed quotations in this interactive, dynamic journal spread. Touchable elements, such as accordion-fold pullouts, allow the pages to unfold gradually and reveal their secrets. She began her pages by applying a basecoat of gesso and then built up several layers of dry-brush effects with acrylic paints, as well as by stampings with a favorite hand-carved spiral motif, using both solid-color and metallic paints. Her confident use of strong color unites the various elements on both pages, and the addition of decorative hole punches presents yet another aspect of visibility as the pages unfold. She presented various photocopied favorite quotations on colorful backgrounds and used a rubber-stamp alphabet set to record a meaningful passage. Strips of copper tape (normally used for stained-glass projects) make a shiny appearance on both pages, dotting a fiber cascade on the left page, and as a method of taping down a moveable fold-down element on the right. Feel-good elements, such as soft tassels of multicolored threads, invite the exploration of these pages and the further enjoyment of the carefully selected words.

SUGGESTED MATERIALS

Acrylic paints

Inexpensive brushes and makeup sponges

Rubber stamps, including an alphabet set

Inkpads

Color photocopies of museum reproductions

Commercial stencils

Fibers and threads

Copper tape

Artist's insights

1 Use pull-out, fold down, and see-through elements. Think of ways to add compartments and hidden sections into your journal pages. Extensive knowledge of the book arts is not necessary, and the spirit of experimentation will take you far.

2 Collect touchable items to add to your journal pages. Buttonhole twist, embroidery thread, artistic fibers and twines, and lightweight wire are just a few possibilities.

Exemplar Journal

ARTIST LYNNE PERRELLA

} *Work a single subject*

Sometimes an entire journal can be devoted to a single subject. In this case, collected visual reference material about alphabets and numerals inspired the artist to create pages of collaged and painted versions of the subject. She began these pages with a coat of white gesso and then used repeated applications of water-soluble pastels to add a basecoat of strong color. She went through her collection of cardboard stencils and experimented with various ways to use the stencils not only to make imprints but also to use as collage elements. To make the pages look like a weathered, peeling billboard, she used heavy overpainting on each stencil and scraped the surfaces

once they had dried. In addition to stencils, she used antique wood type dipped into acrylic paints to imprint some of the letters. Rubber stamps, shipping tags of different shapes and sizes, antique brass letters, and other found objects were also incorporated. She also added a series of numerals. When the pages had dried, she added drips of paint and random splatters of watered-down acrylic paint.

Artist's insight

Collect what you love. If you have an affinity for typography and numerals, start amassing a collection of found letters, such as Scrabble tiles, antique wooden type fonts, dry-cleaning tags, numbering devices from stationery and hardware store aisles, classroom alphabet stencils, and metal salvage-yard finds. Whether you use these objects to imprint a journal page, incorporate them into an assemblage, or feature them as a fascinating still life in your studio, you will be constantly reminded of the beauty and keen design of letterforms.

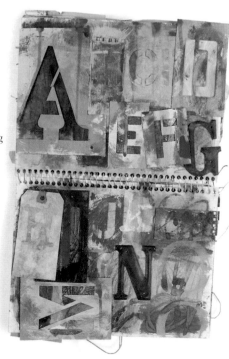

Mica Heart

ARTIST NINA BAGLEY

} *Mixed-media journal page*

When the artist decided to experiment with a new approach to her journals and artist books, she found that simpler was better. With the emphasis on heartfelt words, either from her own pen or from her favorite words of authors, she has discovered a way of using ink-jet transfers on smooth watercolor paper. She also adds notations in her own handwriting with pencil or pen. Once she stabilizes the transfers with a heat gun, both the look and the feel of the page is softer-than-soft. The mica heart, held in place with small strips of cloth, tells a story about "this thing called hope." (See pages 28–29 for more information on transfers of all kinds.)

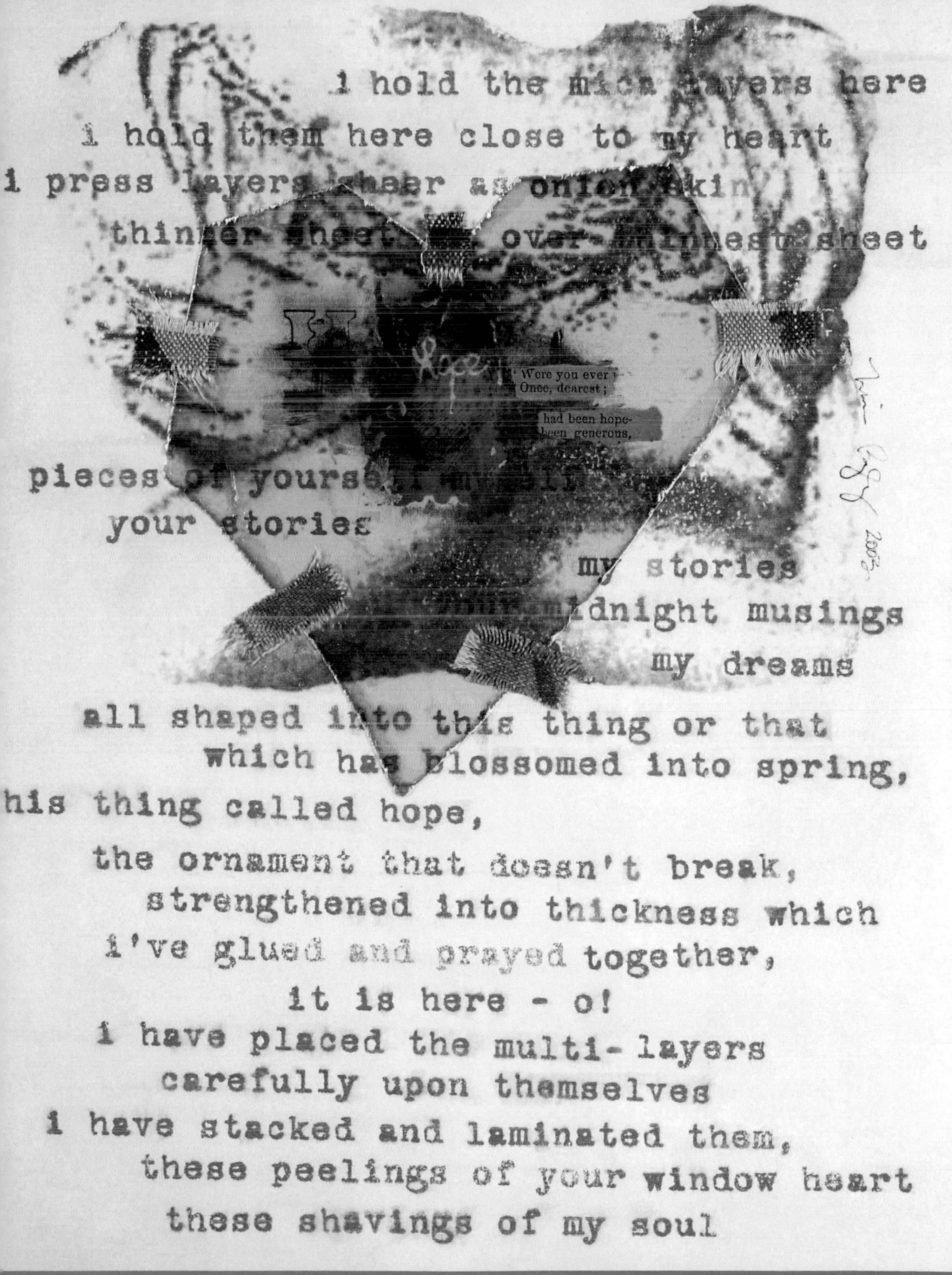

i hold the mica layers here
i hold them here close to my heart
i press layers sheer as onion skin
thinner sheet over thinnest sheet
Hope
Were you ever
Once, dearest;
had been hope-
been generous,
pieces of yourself
your stories
my stories
midnight musings
my dreams
2003
all shaped into this thing or that
which has blossomed into spring,
his thing called hope,
the ornament that doesn't break,
strengthened into thickness which
i've glued and prayed together,
it is here - o!
i have placed the multi- layers
carefully upon themselves
i have stacked and laminated them,
these peelings of your window heart
these shavings of my soul

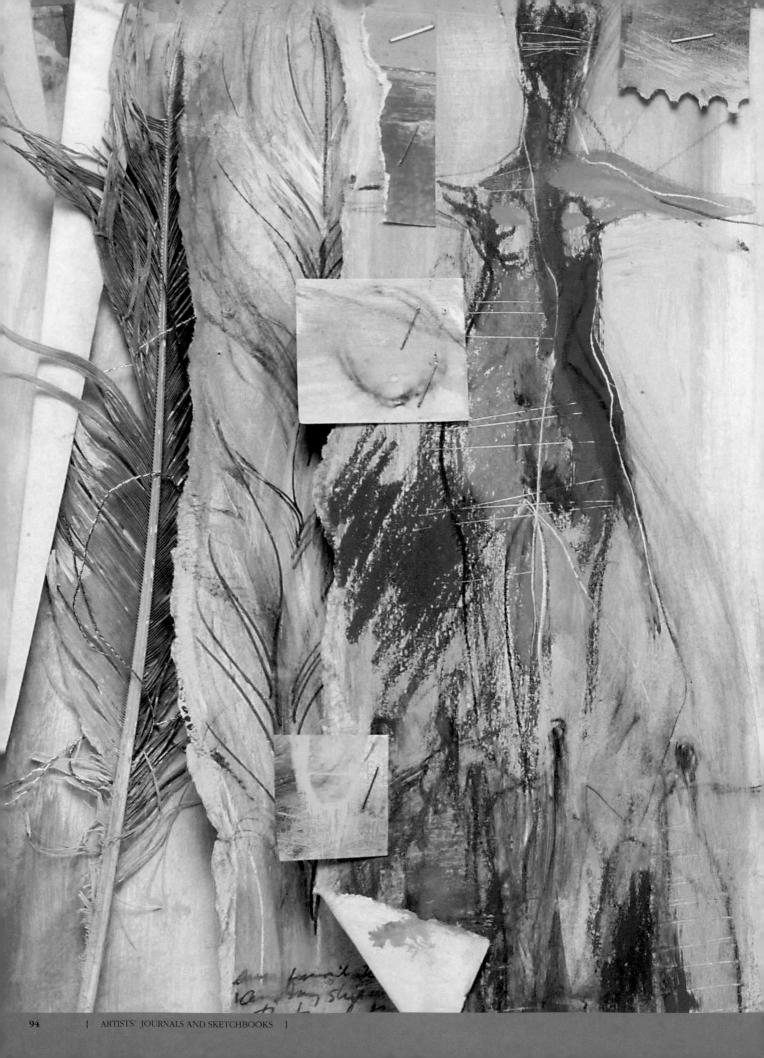

94   { ARTISTS' JOURNALS AND SKETCHBOOKS }

"What is important is not what someone is but what he is waiting for. Not the events of his life but its possibilities"—Dorothee Solle

Icons and Imagery

Keeping an artist sketchbook

I once saw a definitive exhibit of Jackson Pollock's work at the Museum of Modern Art. The show, covering his entire career, included his early student efforts and followed through to his huge, well-known splattered canvases. Although his early paintings were influenced by the realistic approach of his respected instructors, his sketchbooks were full of experimental and iconic markings that were the rumblings of his later signature abstract work. His sketchbook was a place of dreams, a repository for experimental and unguarded thoughts that would later redefine the world of art.

American novelist Jack Kerouac used pocket-size, spiral-bound notebooks to record his impulses and travels across America in the late 40s, and his seminal novel, *On the Road*, comprised passages from these small books. Kerouac saw his notebooks as companions, as well as a place to record strongly felt and instantaneous observations.

Leonardo da Vinci's notebooks became the storehouse for his myriad interests and discoveries and included his notations on subjects ranging from anatomy to zoology. The famous volumes include writings, notations, and plans for churches, palaces, and villas, as well as sketches and studies for his most noted works of art, including *The Last Supper*. The notebooks allowed him not only to explore a subject in-depth, but also to record his realizations and put these into visual form on a page.

Clearly, the term "sketchbook" is open to interpretation.

Einstein Book and Box
} *Sketchbook page*

ARTIST ANNE BAGBY

Waiting in airports can be a boring experience.
To ward off potential wasted time between
flights, this artist created a carry-on art kit
consisting of a biography of Albert Einstein, a
blank sketchbook, drawing supplies, glue
sticks, rubber-stamp alphabets, and a sheaf of
photocopied images of the famous thinker.
Her Einstein-in-a-box sketchbook, created
mostly in airports and hotel rooms, evokes an
Einstein quotation: "Imagination circles the
world." By taking some hints from this artist,
you can be assured that you will never be
without a creative opportunity, even when
circling the world. Assemble a small grouping
of reliable and portable art supplies into
zip-lock plastic bags, and tuck them into a
lightweight carrier, ready to store in the
overhead bin until after take-off. We are often
tempted to take written notes while reading
an especially interesting book, but an
accompanying sketchbook provides another
way of committing the ideas to paper in a
strong, visual, memorable way. Imagine a
whole shelf full of sketchbooks, side by side
with the books that inspired them. Try this
sketchbook technique with a recent book, or
pull out a longtime favorite volume and create
an homage to the book by filling a sketchbook
with free-association drawings and notes.

Decorator's File

Visualizing a design project

One of the most rewarding activities in life is planning and creating a personal home environment. Use your journal as a place to keep the out-of-the-clear-blue-sky ideas that constitute the mythic "house in your head"— that perfect someday home. This design sketchbook is burgeoning with fabric swatches, sample cards, paint charts, and sketches of room arrangements and furnishings. Perhaps you are ready to roll up your sleeves and begin tackling that outdated kitchen with do-it-yourself zeal. To focus your ideas and note some of the potential arrangements on paper, treat yourself to the pleasure of creating a decorator's idea file.

In this sketchbook spread, all the elements of a remodeled kitchen come together. The sketches of the floor plan are surrounded by ideas for window treatments, as well as product samples that were collected on shopping expeditions. Using mostly clips and tape, the artist attached elements in a momentary way, allowing the pages to be constantly updated and changed. She included magazine and catalog clippings, as well as a sketch of the cabinetry. The sketchbook page remains a work-in-progress as more options are considered, and elements are easily replaced or even taped over. A decorator file is a visual way of considering options, a way of gathering numerous visual possibilities to envision a complete room setting. Don't forget your plans for an outdoor area. Sketchbooks are ideal as you formulate ideas for a total landscaping plan or an outdoor living space, such as a deck or gazebo.

Consider starting a decorator's file and sketchbook as a way of not only organizing your plans for an upcoming project but also of celebrating your appreciation for color, texture, and pattern. Work on it gradually, over several months, as you formulate ideas. Keeping track of small details is one of the many roles that a design file can play. Here, the artist's final selections, including sketches of the furnishings and accompanying fabric swatches, have been gathered onto the page, providing a strong sense of what the completed room will look like.

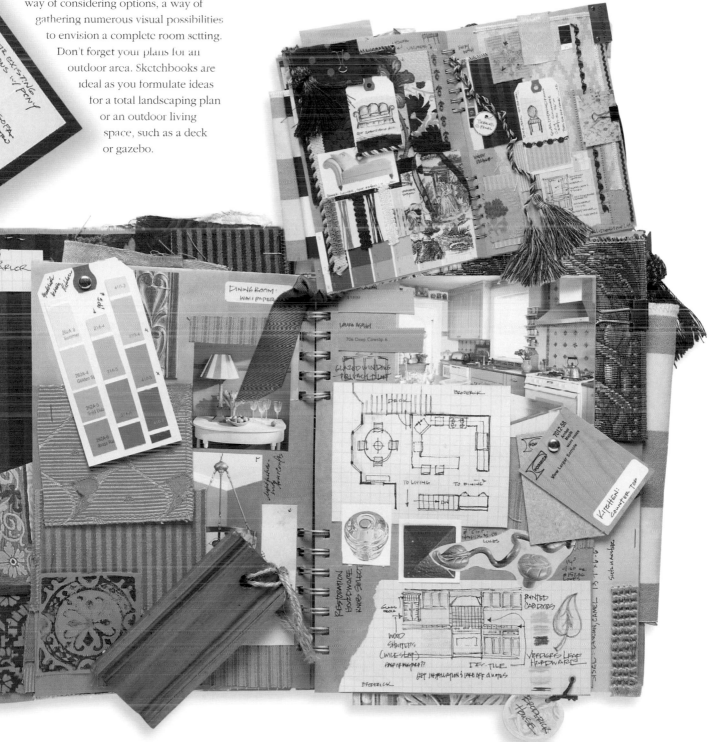

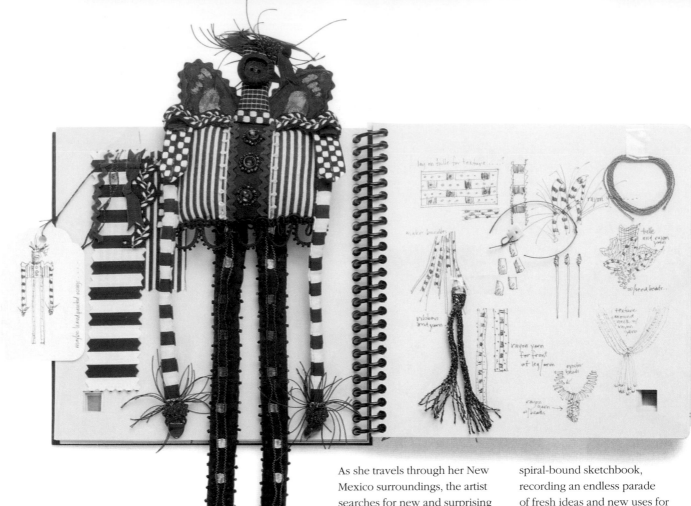

Planning and recording a project

{Amiga con Alas

ARTIST MARIA C. MOYA

As she travels through her New Mexico surroundings, the artist searches for new and surprising materials to use in constructing her unique art dolls, such as small bits of packaging to use for a tiny crown or the wings of a spirited angel. She fills her sketchbooks with small, precise idea drawings, recording the endless possibilities in fine detail and written notations. She begins her notes for a new collection in this compact,

spiral-bound sketchbook, recording an endless parade of fresh ideas and new uses for long-favored materials such as narrow ribbon and rickrack. These notes serve as reminders for sudden impulses that can quickly evaporate. The artist's completed doll rests on the open sketchbook, showing the direct connection between her planning and the final work of art.

Artist's insights

1 Create an idea sketchbook for an upcoming art project. Make notes about your goals, your ideas, and your inspirations. Include sketches and visual reference material that you want to keep close at hand as the project develops.

2 Allow the pages to reflect your creative process as you work through the challenges, as well as new awarenesses, unexpected roadblocks, and major breakthroughs.

3 In addition to sketches, add Polaroid photos of the work in progress, as well as swatches or color chips.

Gathering Italian Colors

ARTIST LINDA BLINN

Creating an onsite sketchbook

Use the materials at hand. This phrase took on a literal meaning for the artist as she worked in a travel sketchbook during her stay at a Tuscan farmhouse. She imprinted her pages with objects as diverse as plants, wine corks, and cut fruits dipped into paint or inkpads. A small table near a window was her command post as she worked quickly with rubber stamps, water-color pencils, stickers, markers, and other sup plies to create this evocative sketchbook page. She recommends inscribing your pages with lists (names of streets, wines, plants, flavors of gelato) to provide creative jump starts as you begin your pages on-site, as well as vivid reminders once you are home.

Artist's insight

Look down—even the sewer covers in an ancient city such as Florence can be inspirational. You may also discover fascinating discarded paper bits to paste onto your sketchbook pages.

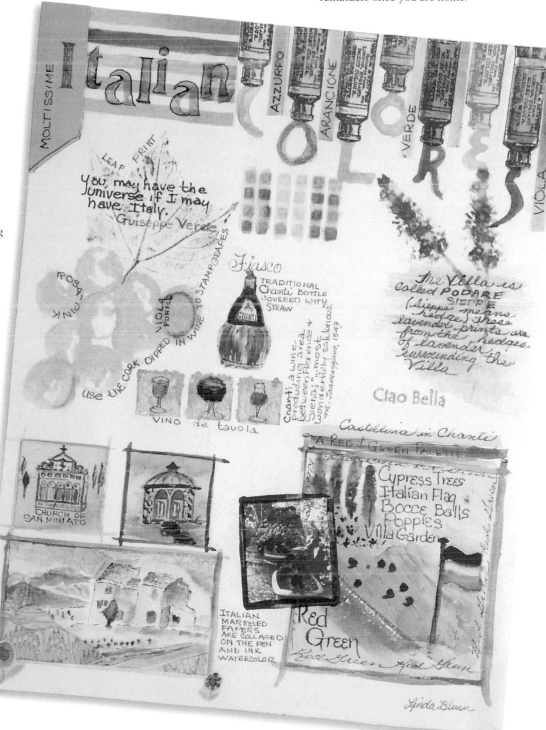

LE MOULIN DES FRES
GRAMAT FRANCE

Hear the buzz of insects and smell the herbs in the kitchen garden. This on-site watercolor sketchbook page evokes the sights and sounds of this small corner of Gramat, France, on an early spring day. Create a sketchbook as a faithful reminder of a particular moment in time that can take you back to these vivid memories at a moment's notice.

Travel Sketchbook

ARTIST JOCELYN CURRY

Watercolor sketchbook

In our daily lives, we seldom make the time to slow down and sketch our surroundings, so the reverie of that activity becomes one of the most treasured aspects of travel. It is worth the time and trouble to research the right book for your travel sketches. Make sure the paper is agreeable for the medium you plan to use, and be sure that the size and shape of your sketchbook is conducive to your style of sketching. Some artists like to add written notations to their sketches. In this case, however, the skillful interpretation of light and shadow and soft greenery against an ancient mortared wall supplies plenty of exposition. The watercolor sketch strikes the perfect balance between what to leave in and what to leave out.

}

*Sketching the
exterior world*

ARTIST PERRY ROLLINS

Italian
Sketchbook

Artist's insight

Art-supply stores and catalogs
offer sets of paints, marking pens,
and brushes, specifically geared to
the traveling artist. However, no
matter how well prepared you are,
you can still be caught without all
the proper sketching supplies.
Never fear—some of the most
successful quick studies are done
with a ballpoint pen on the back
of a utility-bill envelope. Being
receptive to the environment is far
more important than being well
equipped. Seize the moment!

This sketchbook traveled throughout Italy,
recording scenes in Rome, Venice, and (on
these pages) Florence. Using water-soluble,
fine-tipped marking pens, the artist created a
quick first-impression sketch of the renowned
Ponte Vecchio. Although he has ear-marked
this well-traveled sketchbook with diary nota
tions to pass along to his future grandchildren,
his other on-site paintings were popular
enough to be sold, straight from the easel, to
passing fellow admirers of the ancient and
seductive city. Throughout time, artists from
Ruskin to Van Gogh have captured their sur
roundings in sketchbooks, making penciled
notations that helped them recapture and
recall their travels once they returned to the
studio. Consider including a sketchbook in
your luggage each time you leave home, even
for a weekend trip. The quiet moments spent
drawing your surroundings will allow you to
commit the scene to memory and pay silent
tribute to your destination.

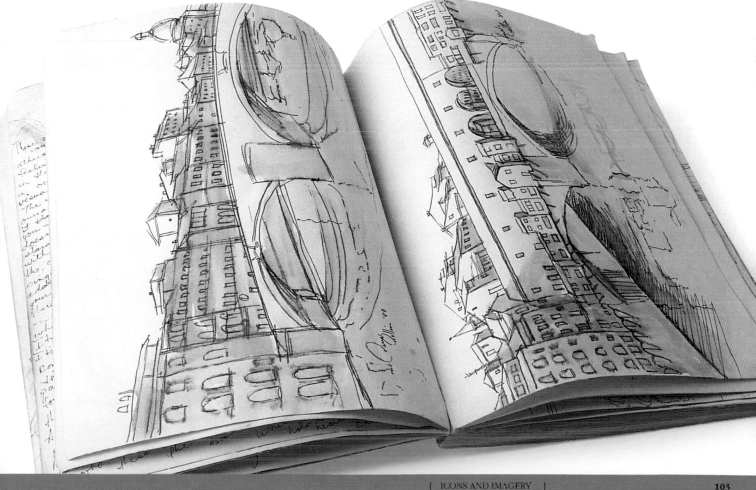

Sketching the *interior world*

Zetti Sketches

ARTIST TRACY V. MOORE

Some sketchbook entries are meant to map the interior world, as opposed to capturing our real surroundings. In this case, the artist has taken "idea" drawings, done on yellow, lined paper, and collaged them to a journal page, continuing to add color, notations, faux postage, and additional markings. The lively page is an accumulation of various sketching sessions, combined for maximum graphic punch. Although visual elements and drawings dominate the page, the addition of diary entries creates a balance between the real world and a fantasy universe. Jottings of phone numbers and reminders about business matters share space with the creatures in the artist's futuristic imagination. He added color with wide-tipped markers and used fine-tipped pens for drawing and diary entries.

When is a sketchbook also a diary and a journal? This hybrid work of art is the invention of the artist, who is currently in her ninth year of creating unique calendars. She invents chronicles of her daily life, using visual symbols. She views her calendars as "an interesting way to document time" and has worked out a series of symbols and icons to describe recurring activities, such as bike rides, yoga, figure-drawing, and studio time. However, sometimes a specific occurrence, such as

wonderful coat," will come along to challenge her to invent a new icon on the spot. In finding this artistic and creative way of documenting her world, she has also invented a powerful new visual language. Although some of her earliest calendars were drawn with pen and watercolor paints, she created her more recent pages with a fine-tipped marker on cardstock.

Drawing *on paper*

Sketchbook/ Diary, October

ARTIST MELANIE MOWINSKI

JOURNALING QUICK TIPS

1. Experiment. Try filling the spaces of your existing desk calendar with daily icons and images that describe your activities and feelings. Use simple art supplies, such as markers or colored pencils.

2. Edit yourself. Find a handful of words that describe your mindset on a particular day. Incorporate them into your desk calendar jottings.

3. A visual calendar may be the perfect way of charting your progress on a particular project (such as a book manuscript) or a challenging goal (such as training for a marathon). By creating your own symbols, you will have a strong visual record of your progress, as well as a lasting document to remind you of your accomplishments.

Expanding the Boundaries

Exploring alternative surfaces and forms

WHEN IS A JOURNAL NOT A JOURNAL?

WHEN IS A DIARY NOT A DIARY?

When we set out to capture an experience, a feeling, a memory, or a visual exploration, the path does not always lead us to work within the pages of a book. We may end up in a woodshop, using hand tools; or at a sewing machine, creating an expressive banner or quilt; or at an easel, painting large colorful canvases. The goal is to find our authentic voice, regardless of the format or medium.

In this chapter, you will see works of art that defy the boundaries of journals or sketchbooks; yet, they possess the same ability to chronicle, document, describe, define, and explore. Taking a "no rules" approach, these artists have used offbeat and experimental materials, combining them to create narrative works of art, including garments and gallery installations. Further, these artists have pushed the limits of the "usual" bookmaking materials, suggesting ways of turning practically any interesting material into a book. Endlessly inventive, each piece tells a story and invites viewers to remain wide awake to their surroundings and serendipitous discoveries.

Step outside your usual creative box and experiment with new materials, techniques, and surfaces, allowing your instincts to take you to a new and fresh experimental vision.

These works of art have an untamed, experimental nature, sort of like Journaling on the Edge—swinging on a creative vine and having confidence that the outcome will be expressive and personal. Whether reclaiming a memory or exploring a dream image, the artists have employed the chosen materials to make a bold statement about a moment in time.

Begin to realize that objects have power and are often the key to unlocking ideas. Place a group of well-loved objects on your drawing board—perhaps some pieces of colored beach glass, a tangle of multihued ribbons or fibers, or a tower of unpainted, wooden cubes. Rearrange the objects, and explore your reasons for collecting these things in the first place. Did you resonate to the colors, textures, or shapes? Perhaps they provided a touchstone to a memory, person, or place? The freewheeling exploration of objects, combined with the "No Rules" dictum of art journaling, is a heady and lively playground where almost anything can happen.

ARTIST SAS COLBY

Taos News Diary

Unbound pages

"Taos News Diary," by artist Sas Colby, is a testament to the beauty of often-overlooked things. She collected streetside detritus from her daily walks and sewed, glued, and painted the humble items onto a background of newspaper covered with gesso and shellac, allowing the items to be considered as talismans. This gallery exhibit, comprising 15 unbound pages, allows us to take a new look at our notion of diaries and chronicles. Consider the possibilities on your next walk and begin to develop a keen eye for the shapes, colors, and intense character of discarded objects, as well as the narrative quality of these throwaway items.

The Seeds of Possibility

Found-object mixed-media book

3½" x 2" x 1¼" (8.4cm x 5.1cm x 3.2cm)

Artists Linda and Opie O'Brien made this one-of-a-kind book from the various parts of a hard-shelled Lagenaria gourd. The artists' love for and appreciation of gourds has led them to thoroughly research the subject and create unique works of art using nature's pottery. It was only a matter of time until they attempted to combine their love of gourds and their flair for artist books and journals. They chose two thick, matching sections of the gourd as covers, and cut out the shapes using a jigsaw (be sure to wear a mask). They then sanded the pieces and applied leather cream to enrich the color. The embellishments on the cover include a hand-fashioned house motif of copper surrounding three tiny gourd seeds and a small watchmaker's vial containing smaller seeds. A vintage bone game piece was used to decorate the spine, and the cascading closures consist of waxed linen thread, leather-hard gourd seeds, and small beads. Handmade paper pulp, including the scrapings from the inside of the gourd, form the pages of the book.

Flight of the
Art Angels

ARTISTS SUSAN SHIE
AND JAMES ACORD

} *Mixed-media
diary quilt*

Have you always thought of quilting as a regimented and daunting art form? Then join "The Lucky School of Quilting Techniques," and get happy. Artists Susan Shie and James Acord have brought their teaching techniques to throngs of appreciative students, encouraging them to create engaging "Outsider Art Quilts." This diary quilt, created as an homage to two kindred artists, stands as a perfect example of what happens when creative quilting techniques are combined with a written diary. Hand-painted, cotton muslin fabric provides a starting point. The artists used Rub-a-Dub laundry markers to write directly onto the fabric—no first drafts or copying from a scripted entry. The heartfelt nature of these diary quilts relies on the direct-from-the-heart immediacy of diary entries, flowing out of the end of a pen. They over-stitched the text afterward using embroidery stitching in contrasting colors of floss or pearl cotton threads. French knots, as well as beads, charms, shisha mirrors, and sequins, are commonly used to punctuate the joyous, colorful surface. Pick up an embroidery needle, and begin a diary entry on painted cloth, keeping in mind the artists' encouraging admonition—Play and be happy.

Journal skirt

Day of the Dead

ARTIST RICË FREEMAN-ZACHERY

Part-garment, part-shrine, this journal skirt by artist Ricë Freeman-Zachery describes her fascination with the colorful traditions of El Dia de los Muertos. A rubber-stamped journal entry describes the day people go to welcome the returning spirits, and a devoted couple of celebratory skeletons wear clothing appropriate to the occasion, rendered in cotton fabrics, embroidery thread, beads, ribbon, braid, and fabric roses. Freeman-Zachery suggests starting the project with a denim skirt, dress, or jacket and planning your additions using paper patterns to determine placement and design of the finished journal garment. She uses permanent-press cotton for appliqués, turning under the seam allowances and using hidden hand-stitches to apply. Use screen-printing ink to imprint the rubber-stamp alphabet letters, and heat-set with an iron after the ink is dry. Bring your love of journaling and personal expression out into the open with a garment meant to celebrate the joy of favorite things.

ARTIST MONICA RIFFE

For Andy

Mixed-media assemblage

Artist Monica Riffe found everything she needed to create this narrative homage to her grandfather in the woodshed of the family's deep-woods rustic camp in Colorado. The assemblage pays tribute to her grandfather, Andy Hansen, whom she shadowed as a child, learning an appreciation for simple, stark, found materials.

Odd, interesting bits from the shed, including an old #2 pencil that may have spent time tucked behind Andy's ear as he worked, are stapled, glued, and tapped together with nails. The construction is not necessarily permanent, but the emotional power of the assemblage is strong and enduring.

my art is the embodiment of my inner Language.

Images unearthed are not merely random they are metaphor.

I am not creating something else.

I am revealing who I am.

2-14-03

in my theatre of dreams

Dream
Theater

ARTIST CATHERINE MOORE

*Mixed-media
assemblage*

Working with the images, colors, and moods of an actual dream, the artist has created this conceptual theater as a stage for presenting dimensional, visual symbols and written journal entries. A black and white harlequin design wraps the outside of the box theater in a traditional pattern, whereas the inside colors depict mystery and quiet. The solitary, faceless figure was hand-sculpted, painted, and draped in loosely woven fabric, which was painted and waxed. Rusted window screen filaments surround the figure as she rests against a canvas stage set with brush lettering, recreating a journal entry. The back wall of the theater features a painted moon against a collaged backdrop of text with a waxed coating.

Rainbow
for Rumi

ARTIST MONICA RIFFE

*Mixed-media
collage*

Bring your favorite quotations out into the open and allow them to illuminate your next mixed-media collage. Flip through your journal pages, and find some favorite words to live by that are too special to remain hidden. Artist Monica Riffe has created this brightly colored collage and surrounded the visual images with words by Rumi, the Persian poet. The rainbow of patterned paper beads seem to describe "pieces of cloud dissolving into sunlight," whereas the postage stamp accents speak of a more earthly universe. Imagine a series of these collaged panels, each illuminating a different verse of a well-loved poem.

Mixed-media journal

}

Why Life Is Sweet

ARTIST LESLEY JACOBS

Not many artists would think to use tin cans to tell a story about the sweetness of life and all of its pleasures, but artist Lesley Jacobs has a graphic designer's eye for spotting strong, colorful graphics wherever she finds them. She enjoyed "scheming and scouring the city for cans" to use in this alternative and unique pocket-size metal journal. Shopping for her supplies took her to various places, including import markets for brightly colored candy tins, a machinist's tool shop for heavy-duty hole punches, a stained-glass supply shop for copper foil tape used to wrap the edges of each page. Many of the attachments to the pages are available at craft or scrapbooking stores, including metal eyelets, "page pebbles," and beveled-glass frames. In addition to words spelled out using purchased letters, the artist suggests using a permanent marker to write across the tin surfaces. Using heavy-duty eyelets and cord to bind her tin pages together, she has used dozens of hard surfaces to tell a story about the lighter and brighter things in life and why it really is so sweet.

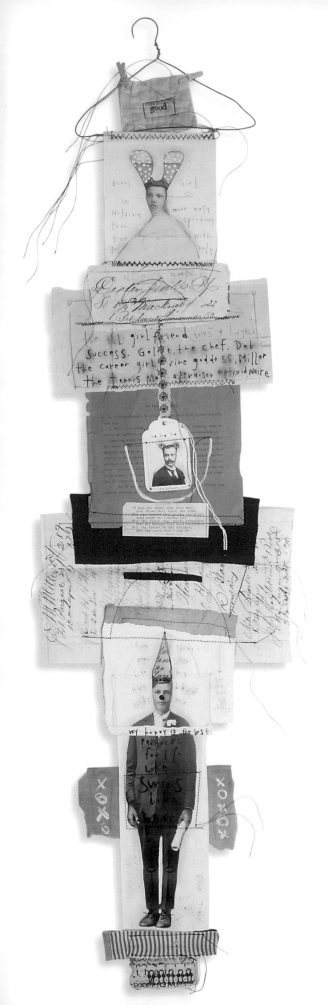

Linear journal

ARTIST LYNN WHIPPLE

Mixed-media assemblage

This delightfully whimsical vertical journal incorporates many of artist Lynn Whipple's signature collage elements with a different twist. She created the diminutive wire hanger as a starting point for the cascading banner of "writing, drawing—all that good stuff." She has combined vintage documents with bits of padded textiles and wisps of old notions, such as a row of hooks and eyes rescued from a forgotten sewing box. She used a sewing machine to stitch the elements together, allowing trailing threads to add a tactile and touchable element to the tender and narrative collage. She added modern-day words using white paint, straight from her brush, to describe the ancestral faces. Old and new are joined by her distinctive flair for storytelling.

Artist Keely Barham combines readily available commercial fabrics with her own computer-generated fabric transfer images to create journal pages that are uniquely tactile and full of saturated color and graphic punch. Glass beads, fabric leaves, and a network of the artist's own stylish stitches and knots provide full coverage for a page that begs to be touched—or maybe even turned into a handbag or wall hanging. For an artist who is equally at home working with paper or fabric, her approach proves that there are no limits when it comes to personal expression.

Flight Dreams

ARTIST KEELY BARHAM

Fabric journal page

It's hard to imagine, but artist Kim Nickens has created the handsome art journal shown here using a host of ordinary desk-drawer supplies. She appropriated computer circuit boards, plus burnished-down lettering, masking tape, and rubber stamps from her own rubber-stamp company, Anima Designs. She also employed her techniques for using metal-etching supplies with transparencies to create a substantial and elegant metal-etched journal cover. More so called ordinary supplies were used for her technique of dying Rives BFK paper with food coloring to create the multitoned book signatures with colored threads in a woven binding.

Metal-Etched Journal Cover

ARTIST KIM NICKENS

Mixed-media art journal

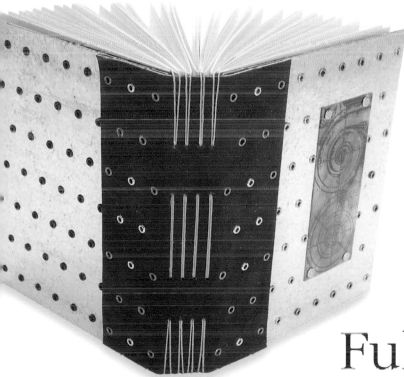

Metal joining plates are used in the construction trade to extend the length of building supplies while adding stability. But in the hands of teaching partners Pam Sussman and Gayle Burkins, the tie plates suggested unlimited possibilities as book covers, with convenient holes (already drilled!) for inserting colorful metal eyelets. Using waxed linen thread, the artists sewed the page signatures to the suede binding with a long stitch. They prepared a copper embellishment by heating it with a microtorch to achieve the mottled and oxidized effect, then imprinted it with a rubber stamp using a black permanent inkpad. They added the embellishment to the book cover using eyelets. Combining offbeat and handsome materials with readily available craft-store supplies, these artists bring a constant flow of new ideas to the traditions of book arts.

ARTISTS PAM SUSSMAN AND GAYLE BURKINS

Mixed-media art journal

Full Metal Jacket

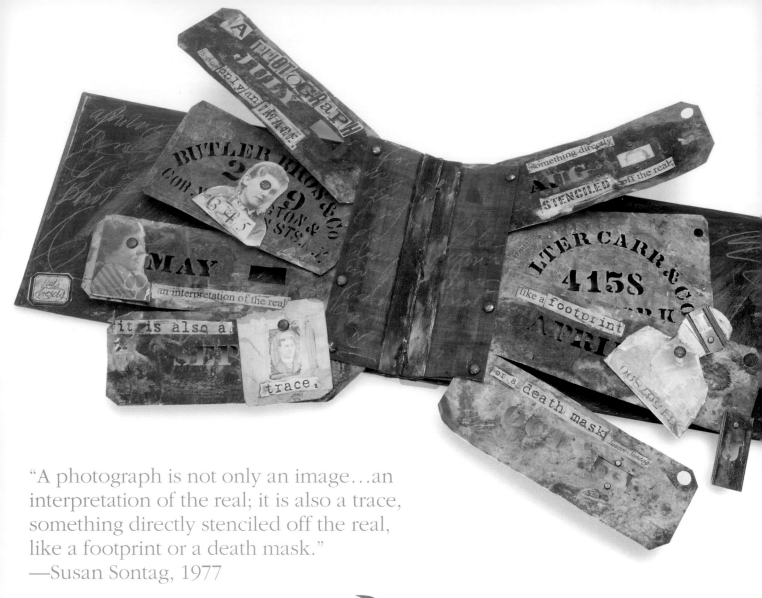

"A photograph is not only an image…an interpretation of the real; it is also a trace, something directly stenciled off the real, like a footprint or a death mask."
—Susan Sontag, 1977

Mixed-media altered book

Alphabets for Draughtsmen

ARTIST JUDI RIESCH

A contemporary writer's words about photography and the artist's love of vintage studio portraits provided the inspiration for this altered book by artist Judi Riesch. The vintage textbook was one step from oblivion when the artist came across it and began her rescue efforts by reinforcing the spine with Tyvek and an application of acrylic paints. The oversized, antique brass stencils, once used for imprinting shipping cartons, have become the pages of the book, fanning out from a central spine of copper mesh fabric. The artist culled the words of the quotation from old books. The antique cabinet photos are applied with gel medium and metal paper fasteners, with added touches of acrylic paints and colored pencils.

ARTIST JOCELYN CURRY

December Diary

} *Mixed-media installation*

Artist Jocelyn Curry captured the essence of her daily walks throughout the month of December 2002, by creating 31 watercolor paper tags, notated with writings, observations, quick sketches of objects collected along the way, and calligraphic letters and numerals. A delicate pigeon feather, a small nugget of beach glass, and a wisp of colored paper are all documented with care, providing reminders of the joy of observation and the celebration of small things discovered and preserved. The completed tags were eventually gathered together and suspended from a 5-foot-long (1.5 meter long) madrona tree branch as part of a gallery installation.

} Contributing Artists

Robin Atkins
837 Miller Rd.
Friday Harbor, WA 98250
USA
Phone: (360) 378-5917
robinatkins@interisland.net
www.interisland.net/robinatkins

Anne Bagby
Winchester, TN
USA
annebagby@bellsouth.net

Nina Bagley
796 Savannah Dr.
Sylva, NC 28779
USA
Phone: (828) 586-1703
ninawitty@aol.com
www.ninabagleydesign.com

Keely Barham
6680 Leafwood Dr.
Anaheim, CA 92807
USA
Phone: (714) 283-2796
FabFrogDesigns@aol.com
www.itsmysite.com/FabricFrogDesigns

Linda Blinn
228 W. Avenida Valencia
San Clemente, CA 92672
USA
Phone: (949) 492-0732
ljblinn@pacbell.net

Sas Colby
2817 Ellsworth St.
Berkeley, CA 94705
USA
Phone: (510) 841-8827
sas@sascolby.com
www.sascolby.com

Juliana Coles
Me & Pete Outlaw Productions
Classes in Extreme Journaling, Workshops,
Original Art
829 San Lorenzo NW
Albuquerque, NM 87107
USA
Phone: (505) 341-2246
meandpete@msn.com
www.meandpete.com

Joceyln Curry
103 N.W. 200th St.
Shoreline, WA 98177
USA
Phone: (206) 546-1877
jcurry@att.net
www.jocelyncurry.com

Sue Nan Douglass
29154 S. Lakeshore Dr.
Agoura, CA 91301
USA
Phone: (818) 575-9967
Phone: (818) 865-0702
suenan@earthlink.net

Lisa Engelbrecht
6329 Mariquita St.
Long Beach, CA 90803
USA
lengelbrecht@earthlink.net

Daniel Essig
111 Grovewood Rd., #3
Asheville, NC 28804
USA
Phone: (828) 251-5554
dessignc@earthlink.net

Sarah Fishburn
119 E. Harvard St.
Fort Collins, CO 80525
USA
Phone: (970) 498-8996
gerety@verinet.com
www.frii.com/~gerety/SarahFishburn

Ricë Freeman-Zachery
Midland, TX
USA
rice.freeman-zachery@att.net
www.voo-doo-cafe.com

Lisa Hoffman
1531 W. 29th St.
Loveland, CO 80538-2469
USA
Phone: (970) 669-6934
lisahoffman@qwest.net

Lesley Jacobs
7728 18th Ave., N.E.
Seattle, WA 98115
USA
Phone: (206) 523-5255
lesleyj@earthlink.net

Linn C. Jacobs
625 N. McCarver St.
Tacoma, WA 98403
USA
Phone: (253) 383-1275
LJacobs262@aol.com

Marylinn Kelly
South Pasadena, CA
USA

Karen Michel
71 Nassau Ln., #3A
Island Park, NY 11558
USA
Phone: (516) 596-4278
Karen@KarenMichel.com
www.karenmichel.com

Jeanne Minnix
12023 Lockett Ridge Ave.
Midlothian, VA 23114
USA
Phone: (804) 594-0842
jminnix@comcast.net
www.jeanneminnix.com

Billye Miraglia
66 N. Sewall's Point Rd.
Stuart, FL 34996
USA
Phone: (772) 286-1736

Catherine Moore
224 Melrah Hill
Peachtree City, GA 30269
USA
Phone: (770) 632-9570
PostoDelSol@aol.com
www.itsmysite.com/CatherineMoore

Teesha Moore
Box 3329
Renton, WA 98056
USA
teesha@teeshamoore.com
www.teeshamoore.com

Tracy V. Moore
Box 3329
Renton, WA 98056
USA
tracyvmoore@hotmail.com
www.zettiology.com

Melanie Mowinski
291 South St.
Williamstown, MA 01267
USA
Phone: (413) 458-7970
moji29@bcn.net

Maria C. Moya
816 Wellesley Dr., N.E.
Albuquerque, NM 87106-1937
USA
Phone. (505) 255-2929
studiomcm@eathlink.net

Brenda Murray
Montreal, Quebec
Canada
bmurray@equilibre.biz
www.brendamurray.net

Connie Newbanks
916 Brookwood Dr.
New Albany, IN 47150
USA
Phone: (812) 945-3739
cndesigns@worldnet.att.net

Kim Nickens
2917 Graham Blvd.
Pittsburgh, PA 15235
USA
Phone: (412) 726-8401
animadesigns@animadesigns.com
www.animadesigns.com

Linda and Opie O'Brien
Burnt Offerings
2170 Evergreen Rd.
N. Perry Village, OH 44081-8703
USA
Phone: (440) 259-2271
gourdart@burntofferings.com
www.burntofferings.com

Lynne Perrella
Acey Deucy
P.O. Box 194
Ancram, NY 12502
USA
aceydeucy1@aol.com
www.LKPerrella.com

Judi Riesch
Philadelphia, PA
USA
jjriesch@aol.com
www.itsmysite.com/judiriesch

Monica Riffe
1903 W. Mulberry
Fort Collins, CO 80521
USA
Phone: (970) 224-9812
monriffe@hotmail.com

Lesley Riley
7814 Hampden Ln.
Bethesda, MD 20814
USA
LRileyArt@aol.com
www.Lalasland.com

Rhonda Roebuck
8476 Mt. Hollow Rd.
Greenwood, VA 22943
USA
Phone: (540) 456-8436
r_roebuck@hotmail.com

Perry Rollins
2405 Route 82
Ancram, NY 12502
USA
Phone: (518) 329-0405
jarol@hotmail.com

Susan Shie and James Acord
2612 Armstrong Dr.
Wooster, OH 44691-1806
USA
Phone: (330) 345-5778
turtles@bright.net
www.turtlemoon.com

Albie Smith
P.O. Box 1927
Jacksonville, OR 97530
USA
papersmith@jeffnet.org

Pam Sussman
228 Ash Ct.
Wexford, PA 15090
USA
PamSussman@aol.com

Michelle Ward
P.O. Box 73
Piscataway, NJ 08855
USA
grnpep@optonline.net
www.greenpepperpress.com

Lynn Whipple
JXLWHIPPLE@aol.com
www.whippleart.com

Resources

Acey Deucy
P.O. Box 194
Ancram, NY 12502
USA
Complete catalog: $5.00
Rubber stamps

Anima Designs
www.animadesigns.com
Rubber stamps, bookmaking supplies,
ephemera

Bonnie's Best Art Tools
Atlanta, GA
USA
Phone: (404) 869-0081
www.coilconnection.com
Coil binders, coils, eyelet punches, book drills,
binding tools

Coffee Break Designs
P.O. Box 34281
Indianapolis, IN 46234
USA
Phone: (317) 290-1542
mikemeador@comcast.net
Eyelets, embellishments, art supplies

Colophon Book Arts Supply
3611 Ryan St., S.E.
Lacey, WA 98503
USA
Phone: (360) 458-6920
Mail-order bookbinding supplies, decorative
papers, marbling supplies

Daniel Smith, Inc.
4150 First Ave., S.
Seattle, WA 98134
USA
Phone: (206) 223-9599
www.danielsmith.com
Papers, art supplies

de Medici Ming Fine Paper
1222 First Ave., #A
Seattle, WA 98101
USA
Phone: (206) 624-1983
Handmade specialty papers

Dharma Trading Company
www.dharmatrading.com
Online source for textile craft supplies

Dick Blick Art Materials
Phone: (800) 723-2787
Call for catalog
www.dickblick.com
Mail-order art and craft supplies

Fanciful's Inc.
1070 Leonard Rd.
Marathon, NY 13803
USA
Phone: (607) 849-6870
www.fancifulsinc.com
Charms, embellishments

Green Pepper Press
P.O. Box 73
Piscataway, NJ 08855
USA
www.greenpepperpress.com
Unmounted rubber stamps, book kits

Claudine Hellmuth
www.collageartist.com

Hollander's
407 N. Fifth St.
Ann Arbor, MI 48104
USA
Phone: (734) 741-7531
www.hollanders.com
Decorative papers, bookbinding supplies,
book cloth, workshops

Home Depot
Check www.homedepot.com for store
locations

Ichiyo Art Center
432 Paces Ferry Rd.
Atlanta, GA 30305
USA
Phone: (800) 535-2263
www.ichiyoart.com
Japanese papers, origami supplies, rubber
stamps

John Neal Bookseller
1833 Spring Garden St.
Greensboro, NC 27403
USA
www.JohnNealBooks.com
Books on calligraphy, book arts, journals,
related supplies

Kinko's
Check www.kinkos.com for store locations

Light Impressions
Phone: (800) 828-6216
www.lightimpressionsdirect.com
Archival photographic and scrapbook supplies

Matthias Paper Corp.
301 Arlington Blvd.
Swedesboro, NJ 08085
USA
Phone: (800) 523-7633
Tyvek and other paper supplies

Ma Vinci's Reliquary
P.O. Box 472702
Aurora, CO 80047
USA
www.crafts.dm.net/mall/reliquary
Rubber-stamp alphabet sets

Michael's
Check www.michaels.com for store locations
Art and craft supplies

Modern Options
www.modernoptions.com
Crafting supplies

Office Depot
Check www.officedepot.com for store
locations

Paper and Ink Arts
3 N. Second St.
Woodsboro, MD 21798
USA
Phone: (800) 736-7772
www.PaperInkArts.com
Inks, pens, tools, books and paper for lettering
and book artists

Paper Source
Check www.paper-source.com for store locations
Domestic and international decorative and handmade papers, rubber stamps, workshops

Pearl Paint Company
308 Canal St.
New York, NY 10013
USA
Phone: (800) 451-PEARL
Call for catalog
Art and craft supplies

Plaid Enterprises, Inc.
3225 Westech Dr.
Norcross, GA 30092
USA
Phone: (800) 842-4197
Acrylic paints, rubber stamps, craft supplies

Portfolio Series Water-Soluble Oil Pastels
www.portfolioseries.com

Ranger Industries
Tinton Falls, NJ 07724
USA
Phone: (732) 389-3535
www.rangerink.com
Ink pads, embossing supplies, crafting specialties

Renaissance Art/Art Keepers
P.O. Box 1218
Burlington, CT 06013
USA
Phone: (860) 283-9237
Rubber stamps, crafting supplies

Rugg Road Paper Company
105 Charles St.
Boston, MA 02114
USA
Phone: (617) 742-0002
Handmade specialty papers, book arts

Staedtler, Inc.
21900 Plummer St.
Chatsworth, CA 91311
USA
Phone: (818) 882-6000
www.staedtler-usa.com
Paints, watercolor pencils, crayons, brush markers, pens

Stamper's Anonymous
25967 Detroit Rd.
Westlake, OH 44145
USA
Phone: (888) 326-0012
www.stampersanonymous.com
Rubber stamps, crafting supplies, workshops

Stampington & Company
www.stampington.com
Rubber stamps, kits, crafting books, supplies

Strathmore Artist Papers
www.strathmoreartist.com

Turtle Press
2215 N.W. Market St.
Seattle, WA 98107
USA
www.turtlearts.com
Rubber-stamp alphabet sets, paper and book arts supplies

Twinrocker Handmade Paper
100 E. Third St.
P.O. Box 413
Brookston, IN 47923
USA
Phone: (800) 757-8946
twinrocker@twinrocker.com

US Artquest, Inc.
Phone: (800) 200-7848
www.usartquest.com
Perfect Paper Adhesive, art and craft supplies

Zettiology
P.O. Box 3329
Renton, WA 98056
Fax: (425) 271-5506
Catalog: $4.00
Online Catalog: www.zettiology.com

International Resources

Bondi Road Art Supplies
179-181 Bondi Rd.
Bondi, NSW 2026
Australia
Phone: 02 9387 3746
bondiroadart.com.au
Art and craft supplies

Collins Craft & School Supplies
Shop 2 / 199 Balcatta Rd.
Balcatta, WA 6021
Australia
Phone: 08 9345 3250
belindacollins@q-net.net.au
Rubber stamps, inks, punches, crafting supplies

Creative Crafts
11 The Square, Winchester
Hampshire, WO23 9ES
UK
Phone: 01962 856266
www.creativecrafts.co.uk

Eckersley's Arts, Crafts and Imagination
Australia
Phone: 1800-227-116
Call for catalog
www.eckersleys.com.au
Art and craft supplies

Gilbert-Jean Booksellers
Lower Level
Left Bank, Paris
France
Art supplies

Graphic Gro
11 arrondisement, Paris
France
Art supplies

HobbyCraft
Stores throughout the UK
Head Office:
Bournemouth, England
Phone: 1202 596 100
Art and craft supplies

Japanese Paper Place
887 Queen St., W.
Toronto, ON M6J1G5
Canada
Phone: (416) 703-0089
Japanese washi and other decorative papers

John Lewis
Stores throughout the UK
Flagship Store:
Oxford St.
London W1A 1EX
UK
Phone: 207 629 7711
www.johnlewis.co.uk
Art and craft supplies

Paper-Ya
9-1666 Johnston St.
Vancouver, BC V6H 3S2
Canada
Handmade and specialty papers

Stampmania
Shop 2, 4 Newra Ln.
Newra, NSW 2541
Australia
www.stampmania.com.au
Rubber stamps, inks, punches, paints, accessories

Wills Quills
Shop 1, 166 Victoria Ave.
Chatswood, NSW 2067
Australia
Phone: 02 9411 2500
www.willsquills.com.au
Exotic papers, bookbinding accessories, journals

About the Author

Lynne Perrella is a mixed-media artist, author, graphic designer, illustrator, and workshop instructor. Her interests include collage, assemblage, one-of-a-kind books, and art journals. She is on the editorial advisory board of two magazines, *Somerset Studio* and *Legacy*, and makes frequent contributions to *PLAY—The Art of Visual Journals*. Her mixed-media artwork has appeared in many books and publications. She conducts creativity workshops at various venues, including Alternative Artfest and Carole Segal's Studio of Fine Art. Her interest in teaching comes from an enjoyment of sharing the creative sandbox with kindred artists and making mutual discoveries in a supportive and enthusiastic environment. Her collages are exhibited in galleries throughout the Berkshires, including the New Britain Museum of American Art. Lynne has owned and operated Acey Deucy Rubber Stamps for the past 17 years. Her catalog features her original illustrations and collage compositions, available as quality rubber stamps. She has been married for over three decades to her husband, John, a hospice nurse. The couple lives in beautiful Columbia County, N.Y., two hours north of New York City.

website: www.LKPerrella.com